THE AUTHOR

Darwin Xavier Gass is a minister of the Evangelical and Reformed Church. He was educated at Catawba College, Salisbury, N. C., from which he received the Bachelor of Arts degree in 1934, and at The Theological Seminary, Lancaster, Pa., from which he received the Bachelor of Divinity degree in 1937. After a successful pastorate in Maryland, he was called in 1940 to the more-than-a-century-old pulpit of Heidelberg Church, Schwenksville, Pa., which post he continues to serve. He has been a frequent contributor to religious periodicals.

THINGS IMPORTANT

THINGS IMPORTANT

BY

Darwin Xavier Gass

W. A. WILDE COMPANY

PUBLISHERS   BOSTON

Copyright, 1945
W. A. WILDE COMPANY
All rights reserved

THINGS IMPORTANT

CONTENTS

PART ONE: THE WAY OF THE CROSS

PART TWO: WORDS FROM THE CROSS

PART THREE: IMPORTANT CHRISTIAN BELIEFS

PART FOUR: THE INCLUSIVE PRAYER

PART ONE

THE WAY OF THE CROSS

I. GLORYING IN THE CROSS

"God forbid that I should glory, save in the cross of our Lord Jesus Christ." Galatians 6:14.

THESE words from the pen of St. Paul have weight, not because of their pious sound, but because they come from one who had been with Christ. He may not have been with Jesus in the flesh, but he had been with Christ in the spirit—even as our fellowship with Christ must be. It is not clear whether any one particular factor was more responsible than others in leading him to this momentous conviction. He could not have read it in a book, and through such a channel annexed it into his own thought. Nor is it likely that someone told him that he ought to think thus. Even though he would have heard the idea from another, he was not the type to proclaim ideas which he had not tested in his own experience. There is nothing to suggest that it was immediately revealed to him on the road to Damascus, when he heard the voice out of heaven say, "I am Jesus."

It appears most likely that St. Paul arrived at the conclusion of the text through the tutorship of experience. While in Athens, he had probably attempted to win converts from among the philosophers by "excellency of speech and of wisdom." Having gained very few, if any, converts by that means, he determined, when he reached Corinth, "not to know any thing among you, save Jesus Christ, and him crucified." We can profit by St. Paul's spiritual struggle; for without a vision of the Cross, we cannot begin to understand the Gospel. Without a Cross the teachings and activities of Jesus would be utter foolishness. Without a Cross the resurrection would have been an impossibility.

We, then, may glory in the Cross because it gives authority to Jesus' teachings. There is probably nothing so void of power as a proclamation of principles for others to follow coming from one who shows no intention of himself attempting to follow them. A herald of ideals for men to follow may fail in some respects, but he must put forth an honest effort to practice that which he preaches if he would have them accepted. Jesus went far beyond all that could conceivably be expected of man. In him can be observed perfect success in practicing the principles proclaimed. Some of the finest evidences of that statement come from the Cross itself. He had taught in one of his parables, "go out into the highways and hedges, and compel them to come in." On the Cross he accepts a repentant sinner into the Kingdom. He had taught, "pray for them which despitefully use you, and persecute you."

On the Cross he prayed that God would forgive those who were responsible for his pain. He had taught unlimited forgiveness; to seventy times seven

—and on the Cross he forgives the mob of murderers because of their ignorance, and because he loved even his enemies. He who had restored children, that the heaviness caused thereby might be lifted from the hearts of their parents; he who had healed the sick and the sinful, bringing them health of body and soul, and demonstrating his concern for the well-being of others—on the Cross, heals the tears of his mother by giving unto her John. These serve to illustrate the manner in which authority was given to that which Jesus was and taught. By his death on the Cross, he put the seal of his precious blood on every word he had uttered, and on every deed he had done. We can therefore glory in the Cross of our Lord Jesus Christ.

We may glory in the Cross because Jesus there shows his total lack of any selfishness. Attempt for a moment to place yourself in his position while on the Cross! There is pain. There is agony. There is a maddening torture. Yet he is thinking of others, and planning for their welfare. It is such an outlook which makes a Cross bearable. This was, of course, characteristic of all his ministry. Always he was giving heed to the will of God and the salvation of men rather than to his own personal security. He was unwilling to misuse his divine power to satisfy personal physical hunger; unwilling to be spectacular to gain a following; unwilling to seek worldly power, when it was his mission to plant the seed of heaven in the hearts of others. He set his face to go up to Jerusalem because he loved his fellowmen more than his own physical life. When offered a crown, he rejected it to keep himself worthy of the crown of thorns.

At all points, the absence of selfish motives stands out in bold relief. While on the Cross, when most of us, under similar circumstances, would have been concentrating on our pain, and wishing that we would have given in to the enemy in order to have avoided the ordeal, he was asking God to forgive those who had placed him there; accepting a sinner into his Kingdom; providing for the comfort of his mother. That mortal man can deny or neglect such a man, yea, such a God, seems almost unbelievable. Some do deny and neglect him. "But whosoever shall deny me before men, him will I also deny before my Father which is in heaven." Jesus gave his all. He has proved himself worthy of full devotion and adoration. We can therefore glory in the Cross because of the selflessness exhibited there.

We may glory in the Cross because there Jesus shows himself to be bigger, and more capable of enduring trials, than any of us. If we were to engage a body-guard, we would in all likelihood engage the services of one bigger and stronger than ourselves. When we seek a guide for life, we want that person to be one who understands our position, and who is big enough and strong enough to help us. It is the Christian's conviction that in Jesus he has such a guide. Should we seek guidance in human relations, Jesus shows us the way of love and forgiveness and service and selflessness. Should we seek guidance in the use of material possessions, he shows us the way of stewardship. Should we seek religious insight, he shows us himself and points us to the Father. He, alone, is a trustworthy guide.

The real test of a guide comes when the road of life is rough and beset with dangers. In looking to the Cross, we can be certain that such a guide is available to us in the person of Jesus Christ. Do we have the feeling that others are seeking cause to find fault with us?—the scribes and Pharisees and elders were continually on Jesus' trail, seeking to catch him in his words. Do we feel that we are abused by our fellowmen?—they spat on Jesus; crowned him with thorns, put a robe on him, and mocked him. Do we feel that we have not received justice?—Jesus' enemies went through the formalities of a trial without the slightest intention of granting him justice. Do friends forsake us?—the treachery of Judas is without equal. Does death puzzle us?—Christ conquered death. The Crucified One has proven himself capable of conquering all trials. He has become victor over all the world. He is big enough and strong enough to be your guide and mine. Let us therefore glory in that Cross on which we behold one capable of guiding us through this life into that life which is eternal.

We may glory in the Cross because it is the evidence of God's love for the world; the evidence of God's love for each of us individually. How familiar to the disciples of the Christian religion are the words, "For

God so loved the world, that he gave his only begotten Son, that whosoever believeth in him should not perish, but have everlasting life." Sacrificial giving is a certain symbol of love. When God gave His Son for the sin of the world, he gave a real sacrifice—no mere figurative sacrifice. Jesus had at one time said, "Greater love hath no man than this, that a man lay down his life for his friends." In consenting to the giving of his own life for the life of the world he demonstrates the availability of the greatest love there is to those who seek to obey his commandments. When God gave His Son, he gave a part of Himself. A worthy human father would much rather bear pain in his own body than see his son bear it. Yet God gave His only begotten Son. In this act, God suffered. There can be no greater love than that which is sacrificially given through the channel of pain; than the love made available to us men from the Cross. "God forbid that I should glory, save in the cross of our Lord Jesus Christ."

As Jesus hangs dying on the Cross, he neither needs nor expects pity from anyone. Adoration and thanksgiving are much more in order. The crosses of wood used by Rome were not likely objects of beauty. But by his being on one of them, Jesus has transformed the Cross into a thing of beauty. We are right, therefore, in constructing our crosses of precious and glittering metals—Christ has touched the Cross with divine beauty. "God forbid that I should glory, save in the cross of our Lord Jesus Christ."

II. TO GO WITH JESUS

"If any man will come after me, let him deny himself, and take up his cross, and follow me." St. Matthew 16:24.

IT is our purpose to consider these words, spoken by our Master, with reference to a few of the things that concern us here and now, in the light of the total picture of his ministry while on earth. Perhaps Goodspeed's translation will open to us new shades of meaning: "If any man wants to go with me, he must disregard himself and take his cross and follow me."

It is very clear that men and women of very different types, backgrounds, and habits, saw in Jesus qualities which were to them attractive and desirable. They saw in him many qualities which were lacking in their own lives. Some desired to go with him; to have similar qualities for themselves. Hardened fishermen put aside their nets to go with him. Men skilled in the unscrupulous public finances of that day wanted to be with him. A woman, who was a sinner, anointed him and kissed his feet and found peace. A young ruler saw in him the secret of eternal life and made inquiry. Innumerable persons saw in him the power to overcome physical handicaps. It ought to be to our advantage to note some of the qualities sought by men today which may be found in him.

In him we observe *perfect understanding*. He understood himself: who he was; what he must do; how he must do it. He understood those with whom he came in contact: their motives; their longings; their willingness to supply that which was essential for overcoming obstacles and reaching goals. He understood nature, and the material things with which all are surrounded. This perfect understanding was his because in all things he looked first to God, and then viewed all in the light of God's truth. If we want to go with Jesus in the way of better understanding, we must do likewise.

In him we observe *perfect freedom*. Never is there any hesitancy or fearfulness. He had permitted himself to be bound to God, rather than to men. Much of the lack of freedom felt in the world today can be traced to the fact that the chief bonds were with men, rather than with God. If we desire a healthy lack of restraint; if we want to go with Jesus in the matter of freedom, we must allow ourselves to be in bondage to God.

> "Make me a captive, Lord,
> And then I shall be free;
> Force me to render up my sword,
> And I shall conqueror be."

In him we observe *perfect love*. In spite of the fact that most of us have, at one time or another, seemingly derived some satisfaction from hating something or somebody, we would all, in the quiet moments of honesty, surely admit that it is more pleasant to love than to hate. When the enemies of Jesus criticized him for having fellowship with sinners, which was a manifestation of his perfect love, we cannot help but feel that envy and jealousy were at the root of their criticism. Jesus was capable of winning sinners because he loved them while they were yet sinful. The leaders of the Jews had lost the capacity to win outcasts back into respectable society and religious circles, because they were without love for them. As men are often prone to do, these criticized Jesus as a cover for their own lovelessness. Jesus, on the other hand, had permitted the Spirit of God to rest upon him. If we would go with Jesus in the matter of love, so that the joys of loving even our worst enemies could be ours, we must allow the Spirit of God to dwell within our hearts to direct us.

In him we observe *perfect composure*. He was calm and serene, in manner and appearance, at all times. This is especially noticeable at the time of his trial. When in the presence of the high priest, Jesus had been struck by an officer for an answer given. "Answerest thou the high priest so?" said the officer. "Jesus answered him, If I have spoken evil, bear witness of the evil: but if well, why smitest thou me?" Such is perfect composure! When the silly and irresponsible Herod questioned Jesus, Jesus answered him nothing. This, again, is an example of perfect composure. After Pilate had scourged Jesus, and upon presenting him in the purple robe, crowned with thorns, even the weak-kneed Pilate was forced to say, "Behold the man." Jesus was certain of God's justice and had naught to fear from any man. He knew that man could not, in any real sense, do him harm, and he stood before the world, an example of perfect composure. If we want to go with him in this matter, we must be sure in our hearts of God's love and justice, remembering that "whatsoever a man soweth, that shall he also reap."

It is true that going with Jesus in such matters as affect our daily lives is attractive when our eyes are fixed on the result. Going with Jesus would bring many desirable things—things that practically everyone wants. Yet many in the world refuse to go with him. Like the selfish young ruler who wanted eternal life, they do not desire the things that they want with sufficient intensity to pay the price. These, too, go away sorrowing. It is a law of life; we can reach no destination without traveling the road that leads to that particular destination. It is stated clearly in our text that if anyone wants to go with Jesus, he must deny or disregard himself; he must take up his cross. "For whosoever will save his life shall lose it: and whosoever will lose his life for my sake shall find it."

One way of describing this denial of self is to say that we must discipline ourselves. Discipline has become a bit unpopular—especially discipline from the outside—but much good may come of it, provided we learn thereby to discipline ourselves. Friendships and harmonious fellowship come to an end when the tongue is not disciplined. Disease eats the body when certain appetites and physical urges are not disciplined. The soul perishes when not disciplined in the way of life. How many opportunities for deepening the devotional life, enriching our communion with God, and receiving the blessing which results from worshipping in the house of prayer have been missed through the lack of self-discipline in the matters of arising on Sunday morning, laying aside the newspaper, or turning off the radio! Only God knows how many souls would make steps forward in the matter of going with Jesus, if they would discipline themselves in these simple little things.

Another way of describing self-denial is to say that it is a feeling of detachment from our surroundings. It is a case of being in the world, but not of the world. A man carrying a cross up the hill of the skull was really a detached person. He was in the world, but not of the world in the sense that the observers were. The detached person enjoys the material things of life and its various companionships, but he is not attached to them in such a manner that he would go to pieces if he could no longer have them.

Another description is that of suffering cheerfully if need be. The same burden or suffering, placed on the shoulders of two different persons, may cause one to go to pieces, while the other bears it cheerfully and comes out victorious. The difference is on the inside of the two persons. One sees only the suffering and the burden. The other looks to God, through the Cross of Jesus, and fixes his mind on the goal of being with Jesus. He sees opportunity to deny himself some personal pleasures and satisfactions for a season, that he may reap the greater joys and satisfactions that come from going with Jesus. It may even be that the forces of evil—the powers of sin—shape the cross. It is often so. It was so with Jesus. That need make no difference. "If any man will come after me, let him deny himself, and take up his cross, and follow me." Going with Jesus has many more attractive features than the world can offer, but no one gets there unless he follows the right road: the way of him who is The Way.

III. WHEN IS A CROSS A CROSS?

"If any man will come after me . . . let him take up his cross . . ." St. Matthew 16:24.

THERE are angles from which the Cross is not a pleasant fact to behold, yet, when seen in its totality, it is the most revealing incident in the history of the world. There the fullness of God's love is revealed to a world steeped in sin. There, amid the blackness, the pure in heart see the beginning of a new day.

This matter of taking up one's cross is an obligation which falls daily upon the devoted disciple of Jesus Christ. There is danger, however, that we may be inclined to term various sufferings, inconveniences, and headaches *crosses,* when in reality the term cannot properly be applied to them. All have probably been guilty of at some time terming some thing a cross which did not deserve such label. It is necessary to look humbly to the Cross of Jesus Christ for a clearer insight and a deeper understanding of when a cross is a cross. By giving attention to the outstanding characteristics of Jesus' Cross we may better understand what things constitute a cross for us.

We note first that Jesus' Cross resulted from a miscarriage of justice. That is to state the case mildly, for law and justice were given a holiday when he was condemned. All principles of law and legal procedure were set aside. His was a mock trial if ever there was one. The Sanhedrin could try capital cases only at their regular meeting place; not in the palace of the high priest. Such a trial could not begin during the night, nor even in the afternoon. An elaborate system of warning and cautioning witnesses was provided. How glaring a departure was Jesus' trial from the regular procedure! Of course, the Sanhedrin did not formally pronounce him worthy of death. But to insist on this observation would be to engage in a meaningless toying with words. When presented to Pilate, it was theoretically for trial and not as one condemned. When Pilate suggested trial by Mosaic Law, the accusers excused themselves—which lends emphasis to the fact that they had acted as Sanhedrinists, if not formally as the Sanhedrin. Upon examination of Jesus, Pilate found no fault in him, yet permitted and authorized the crucifixion. It was as though one of our present-day courts should try a man, pronounce him innocent, and then proceed to authorize that man's confinement in prison. One mark of a cross is injustice.

A second characteristic is that Jesus accepted the Cross willingly. It will be recalled that when the armed band appeared to seize Jesus, Peter struck a servant of the high priest, cutting off his ear. After commanding Peter to put up again his sword into its place, he makes this statement: "Thinkest thou that I cannot now pray to my Father, and he shall pres-

ently give me more than twelve legions of angels?"
Powers at his command were not summoned for personal protection. He was offering a sacrifice, bearing
a cross, and doing it because he wanted to—rather
than simply resigning himself to something commanded by another. The same thought—his willingness—is beautifully recorded by St. John: "Therefore
doth my Father love me, because I lay down my life,
that I might take it again. No man taketh it from me,
but I lay it down myself. I have power to lay it down,
and I have power to take it again. This commandment have I received from my Father." Had he been
a poor helpless mortal, we would pity him. But as the
Christ of God and powerful, we admire his manly
courage as he sets out to bear an unjust death willingly. This is not to suggest that we should seek injustice rather than justice for ourselves. There must
be point and reason to the willingness to bear an injustice. This brings to our attention a third observation.

Jesus suffered the Cross for a worthy purpose. There
is no hint of pain for pain's sake. "As Moses lifted up
the serpent in the wilderness, even so must the Son
of man be lifted up: that whosoever believeth in him
should not perish, but have eternal life." St. Paul
speaks of "our Lord Jesus Christ, who gave himself
for our sins, that he might deliver us from this present
evil world, according to the will of God and our
Father." And again, "Christ loved the church, and
gave himself for it . . . that he might present it to

himself a glorious church." In each of these quotations we note that a high purpose motivated Jesus Christ. It was for a worthy end that he suffered. He took up the Cross for our sins—that we might have forgiveness; for the church—that it might be glorious; for us—that we through true faith might have eternal life.

And lastly, we note that an unfailing trust in God permeated the whole experience. One does not pray who does not trust God. Jesus had prayed in the Garden that the cup might pass from him, but God replied in the negative, as he must often reply to many of our prayers—and Jesus accepted the answer of God: exhibiting thereby his great trust. The utterances from the Cross begin and end with prayer. "Father, forgive them: for they know not what they do." At the end: "Father, into thy hands I commend my spirit." Between these prayers he offers Paradise to a penitent sinner, makes provision for his sorrowing mother, and utters a prayer which must be listed as a hard saying—"My God, my God, why hast thou forsaken me?"—but which has its proper place in the total scene. It is addressed to God, whom he trusted even in the darkest moment.

When we remember that Jesus' Cross resulted from a miscarriage of justice; was borne willingly, without any thought of complaining; was borne for a high and worthy purpose; and was borne with an unfailing trust in the goodness of God, we will be less inclined to mark trivial things with the sign of the blood-stained Cross. That portion of suffering which comes by the operation of justice is never a cross. The crucified thieves suffered justly. That portion of disease resulting from our own sin is not a cross. If we resent our pain, and curse the hand which placed it upon us, it loses all power to be a cross and the instrument for spiritual growth. But if an unjust burden is borne graciously for God and our fellowmen, God will not forsake us, nor deny to us his heavenly benediction.

PART TWO

WORDS FROM THE CROSS

I. THE FIRST WORD

"Father, forgive them; for they know not what they do." St. Luke 23:34.

THE words which first fell from the lips of our Lord after the nails which pinned him to the Cross had pierced his flesh would sound extremely unnatural if credited to another. Surely there are very few other men, if any, whose first thought, under similar circumstances, would have been so totally empty of self-concern, and so fully devoted to the spiritual well being of the persons who were apparently least worthy. Yet coming, as they do, from the Master, these words are natural, unforced, and abounding in healing power. "Father, forgive them; for they know not what they do."

His hour had come. He is being baptised with the baptism which he had previously envisioned. He is drinking the cup; drinking all of it—consuming even the dregs. It is a difficult moment for him. There was pain of the flesh. But such pain as can come through the flesh was out-weighed by the pain that was within his spirit when he looked upon the multitudes who at that moment were on trial before God. They had crucified the Son of God. Their words and acts and motives marked them for condemnation. To the gaze of the anointed of God, they must have been a pitiable sight. And of the many needs which they unknowingly had, their most immediate need was of forgiveness.

Realizing their great need, Jesus lifts up both heart and voice to God. Without hesitation, and with ease that must have been apparent to all, he addresses God as Father. Such ease, in this his hour, came not from the moment. It came from the long and continuous and satisfying communion held with God during the days and years of which this was the fruition. Father! Often he had addressed God as Father. He had taught his followers to begin their prayer, "Our Father." Now, seeing men in great need, and presented with the most dramatic incident in his career for exemplifying his Saviourhood, he calmly addresses a simple but far-reaching intercession to the Father. "Father, forgive them; for they know not what they do."

Forgive! For whose forgiveness is he praying? The soldiers who executed the orders of their superiors were closest at hand. Their hands had placed the nails and given them the blows that sent them through his flesh and into the wooden cross-beam. Just beyond the line of soldiers was the mob of tormenters—the tormenters whose minds were not their own, but were under the spell cast by unrighteous men whose motives grew out of the desires of the flesh. Beyond those within the immediate range of human sight were the chief men of Israel, the Roman governor, and him who proved traitor to the Kingdom. "Father, forgive them."

But is it for these alone that he prays? The crucifixion is an eternal fact; he was slain from the foundation of the earth. The prayer for forgiveness is likewise an eternal prayer. It is a prayer which touches all men throughout all time. It is a prayer for which each of us must needs be thankful. Our sins are often like unto their sins. We thoughtlessly give heed to the counsel of those who seek to crucify our Lord. We stand at times in the company of those who mock, allowing their words and acts to influence us until we are ourselves not obviously at variance with them. We follow too often the easier path of personal comfort, rather than sacrificially yielding to the demands of truth.

Over against all this, there is a rather remarkable fact undergirding Jesus' prayer. He had faith in man's capacity to rise above his present level, no matter how low that level might be. That faith had been characteristic of his ministry. Much of his effort had been directed toward those who had been given up by the respectable citizenry as hopeless. To the woman taken in adultery, he said, "Go, and sin no more." He had faith in her capacity to rise above the low level on which she was then living. Whatever our level, there is yet higher ground. His faith in us to move higher is essential. We need to feel that someone has faith in us. Without such knowledge few can rise. To each of us there comes steadying stimulus when we hear the word from the Cross, "Father, forgive them; for they know not what they do."

The basis for Jesus' request works havoc with human pride. Ignorance is no excuse in the eyes of the law. And legal principles reflect the general feelings of the populace. Most persons would rather find any other excuse for an unacceptable act than ignorance. Man takes pride in what he knows. How many of those involved in the crime of the crucifixion took advantage of the forgiveness made available through Jesus' prayer we do not know. It seems very unlikely that those few individuals who were particularly anxious to put an end to Jesus could have sacrificed their pride. They had too much of it. But it is not improbable that some of the mob later came to be disciples. A Roman centurion is quoted as saying, "Truly this was the Son of God."

"They know not what they do." This was most true of the Roman soldiers. They may have been totally ignorant of all the proceedings. As servants of the government, they had received an order. In obedience to their government, they executed the order. Many in the mob did not comprehend the significance of their acts, and they probably cared less. And the more one tries to picture the thought-forms of those in authority, the less likely it appears that they knew what they were doing. Jesus very clearly implies that they did not know what they were doing. They were possessed of religious insanity and moral stupidity. St. Peter later reechoes the same thought when, referring to the crucifixion, he says, "And now, brethren, I wot that through ignorance ye did it, as did also your rulers." St. Paul likewise writes in the same vein, "Which none of the princes of this world knew: for had they known it, they would not have crucified the Lord of glory." And how alarmingly often, even in this day, there must be written over the affairs of the world an epitaph which ought to stir the Church to mighty action—"Religious insanity and moral stupidity." If we truly knew God, we would not sin; even as Jesus knew God and did not sin.

The first word from the Cross comes to us as the seal and signature to a document which was being written throughout the years of active ministry. With every human reason for condemning the persons whose sin had brought him to this painful incident, all condemnation is withheld so long as there is hope of their finding forgiveness. Mahomet, lying wounded at the battle of Ohod, shouted: "How shall the people prosper that have treated thus their Prophet, who calleth them unto their Lord! Let the wrath of God burn against the men that have besprinkled the face of His Apostle with blood!" Then is added this curse: "Let not the year pass over them alive." How different the atmosphere surrounding the crucifixion of our Lord! During his ministry he had said: "Love your enemies, bless them that curse you, do good to them that hate you, and pray for them which despitefully use you, and persecute you."

On the Cross that teaching receives the seal and signature of his blood when he prays, "Father, forgive them; for they know not what they do."

The intercessory character of this brief prayer needs also to be noted. Jesus is not only the lamb led to the slaughter. He is the Christ performing a duty belonging to his office of High Priest. He is showing himself to be the mediator between the perfect love of God and the sin of man. Without his mediatorial activity there is a great void separating man and God. Here we see that void bridged. Man's case is pleaded before God. Man is brought to God, and God is brought to man. The ignorance of man, which is itself a form of sin, is exhibited in bold relief on the Cross by the blameless one's having been slaughtered. It is permitted that we may all see the horror of our misdoings, and turn from them. For if we see sin as it really is, its power over us will be broken. Thus the day-light of God's love is able to shine through and illumine our hearts. Sin is to the soul as a deadly disease is to the body. Yet there is a cure for sin. Forgiveness is the cure which sets us on our feet, thus providing another opportunity. Christ on the Cross, speaking the words of the text, mediates the cure.

When we today look upon the Cross, we see it in a truer perspective than the mob must have seen it at the moment. We see it through the knowledge of all the benefits that have resulted. To the large majority of the mob, the Cross must have appeared as a symbol of defeat. The Church knows it to be a symbol of victory. But even at the moment, some who were spiritually alert may have caught the ring of victory which was in the words of him who looked down from the Cross. Although nailed to the Cross, he was still in command. He had power to either curse or bless. By using his power to intercede for man's forgiveness, he showed himself to be, beyond all doubt, the true Son of God, the Saviour of the world.

II. THE SECOND WORD

"Verily I say unto thee, Today shalt thou be with me in paradise." St. Luke 23:43.

THIS second word from the Cross comes to the Christian most forcefully when viewed in the light of the total setting. Although there is one Cross that towers high over all the wrecks of time, the total crucifixion scene contains three crosses. Two of the crosses hold, as their victims, men whose lives were stained with crime; men who were receiving the just, although cruel, reward for their anti-social conduct. And even in the hour when they are about to die, the ugliness of their character shows forth through the utterances of disdain which they cast at Jesus. It is recorded that people passing by reviled the Lord, saying, "Thou that destroyest the temple, and buildest it in three days, save thyself. If thou be the Son of God, come down from the cross." Likewise the chief priests mocked him, saying, "He saved others; himself he cannot save. If he be the King of Israel, let him now come down from the cross, and we will believe him. He trusted in God; let him deliver him now, if he will have him: for he said, 'I am the Son of God.'" Then St. Matthew adds, "The thieves also, which were crucified with him, cast the same in his teeth."

It will be remembered that not so long before Jesus had said, "And I, if I be lifted up from the earth, will draw all men unto me." How remarkably soon the power of his drawing force exerted itself! A dying criminal on a neighboring cross is caught within the orbit of Jesus' attractive power, and is drawn to the eternal Christ. At the same time another criminal, just as near to Jesus in physical distance, remains unattracted to the Lord of Salvation. Death, which is the wage of sin, remained his master until the end, leaving him without comfort and without hope. Thus the three crosses outline in bold relief a Saviour, a saved man, and a lost man. The world is ever reminded by these three crosses that there is a great stream dividing the good and the evil. For each individual soul that stream grows wider and deeper and swifter with the passing of the moments and the years. There comes a time when to cross the stream is a very hazardous undertaking, although some few do succeed in crossing at the eleventh hour. The penitent thief to whom the second word from the Cross was addressed was one such person. We rejoice in his good fortune, but lament his delay.

Of the two thieves crucified with Jesus, our chief concern is with him who was penitent. His name, according to tradition, was Dysmas, and his crime insurrection. There is every reason to give credence to the tradition concerning his crime. That would also have been the only conceivable charge against Jesus from the Roman standpoint—the Romans would

have been unmoved by the charge of blasphemy. The
day which we have come to call Good Friday would
have been, then, to the Romans, a day on which
several insurrectionists were crucified. That the male-
factor is termed a thief neither adds to nor detracts
from the possibility of his having been an insurrec-
tionist. Very often the bands set upon the destruc-
tion of Roman rule were in practice thieves and
murderers. Whatever his crime, it was such that he
himself recognized the justice of his death on a cross.

He had been hardened by years of crime; he had
joined the mob who sneered; but the words of their
mockery, and his, were burning their way into his
heart. "Son of God." "He saved others." It is as
though the enemies of Christ were preaching the
Gospel of God. A sense of justice begins to dawn on
the thief. He recognizes the justice of his own death,
and the injustice of Jesus' death. He goes beyond that
and envisions the Messiah, the Christ, in the crucified
Jesus. He is moved by the manner in which Jesus
bears the agony of a cruel death; even as the world
today takes notice of the manner in which Church
members stand by their convictions in the hour of
misfortune. Might not there be a possibility that one
who could so easily rise above the suffering of a cross,
and pray in self-less sincerity, could also overcome
death? Would not one who had shown such great love
speak a word of comfort to even a sinner? Such must
have been the vision, the thoughts, and the questions
which flashed through his heart and mind with

lightning rapidity. Helpless to do otherwise, he speaks: "Lord, remember me when thou comest into thy kingdom." He thus became the first fruit of the Cross—the first to accept the forgiveness made available through the prayer and sacrifice of Jesus.

We today who consider faith difficult need to stand for a season and gaze upon two crosses; the Cross of Jesus and that of the penitent thief. The thief had no knowledge of Easter morning to guide his view of the Cross next to his. He saw only a man who claimed to be the Son of God crucified, bleeding, and dying. I fear that too few modern Christians, with their admiration for power and fortune, would have joined the request of the penitent sinner. It would have been easy to mock, as did the mob, and as did the impenitent thief. Yet we can take courage and gain strength for our Christian confession by recalling the cry of the thief. He had to overcome a jungled background and nauseating surroundings. He did it! How much more should we be able to rise to greater heights of faith!

"Verily I say unto thee, Today shalt thou be with me in paradise." The hope of the thief was without doubt for remembrance in a kingdom such as he had been taught during childhood would come to the Jewish people through the Messiah. The only kingdom of which he could conceive was to him something entirely future: "When thou comest into thy kingdom." Having accepted the penitent thief, Jesus opens to him new knowledge and present comfort.

Not in some future and uncertain time will the kingdom become a reality—the kingdom is now a reality. "*Today* shalt thou be with me in paradise."

This word from the Cross has in times past been the center around which the imagination of man constructed numerous celestial geographies. Seemingly, that about which least is known becomes the most fascinating to the imagination. And since there is no basis for any detailed knowledge of what paradise is, many have felt free to read into the word their own preconceived notions as to what it should be. Quite obviously, paradise is not heaven in its fulness, for it was not until later that Jesus ascended into heaven. Yet Jesus says to the penitent thief, "*Today* shalt thou be *with me* in paradise." But on what Scriptural grounds can man make of paradise a purgatory or any of its modifications? It appears quite reasonable that the long dwarfed spirit of the thief would stand in need of growth, and that opportunity for such growth would be provided in paradise. But it does not appear likely that the other thief or any person not destined for heaven should find their way to paradise for another chance in the world beyond. The familiar parable of Dives and Lazarus bulwarks such a statement.

The word 'paradise' itself means a garden or park, especially one surrounding a palace. It may therefore be viewed as that part of hades, the abode of the deceased, surrounding heaven, where those destined for heaven are in joy and bliss as they await the great day when the full splendor of the heavenly glory will be made manifest to them. But even this is of minor significance. The great truth contained in the second word from the Cross, aside from the comfort which it brought to the penitent thief, is that we shall be with Christ.

"Thou shalt be with me," therein lies the secret of true bliss. Whoever has come to believe on the Christ of God, who trusts him for salvation, who loves and serves him, needs no other knowledge. If we have accepted the Crucified One as our personal Saviour in this life, we will be of such a heart and mind as to desire his presence above every other thing, no matter where he may lead us. Any great concern about the geography of the land beyond is foolishness to him who has the assurance that Christ will be with him.

The attitude which compels us to be more concerned about being with the Lord than about the precise nature of paradise puts us in direct spiritual relationship with the early Christians. It is written that St. Stephen, while being stoned, prayed, "Lord Jesus, receive my spirit." Likewise St. Paul writes of his "Desire to depart, and to be with Christ."

Often we are thieves upon a cross. God has granted to us the blessing of life with its many benefits and abundant possibilities. These we gladly accept, and go on our way forgetful that there must be paid the price of thanksgiving and good works. We stand empty handed before the God of justice, and are in need of crying, "Lord, remember me when thou comest into thy kingdom." It is as much to us today as to the thief of yesterday that our Lord replies, "Today shalt thou be with me in paradise."

III. THE THIRD WORD

"Woman, behold thy son! . . . Behold thy mother!"
St. John 19:26, 27.

In this third word from the Cross, Jesus directs both his own and our attention to two sorrowing persons who stood by. These were in company with others, but were singled out for special recognition. A brief word is addressed to one, his earthly mother: "Woman, behold thy son!" To the other, John, the beloved disciple: "Behold thy mother!"

Only a mother can begin to fully appreciate the thoughts and feelings that weighed upon Mary as she stood beneath the Cross. Her first-born crucified like and with the lowest of criminals! There came to her memories such as are common to every mother: memories of his infancy and childhood, when he was dependent upon her; memories of holding him close to herself, soothing his aches, and tucking him into bed with quieting lullaby. Now she beheld him dying. There would come to her memories that must be counted as unusual; memories of the night in Bethlehem when there was no room in the inn, and they were compelled to retire to a stable; memories of a hurried flight to Egypt, so that the infant's life would not be taken by the hand of Herod; memories of their search for him in Jerusalem when he was a lad of twelve; memories of unnumbered moments when her heart was tried, and she never quite understood. Now she stands on a wind-blown hill outside the holy city, her hair grey, her brow wrinkled, widowed, lonely, and cold. It may be that she recalled the words of Simeon, "yea, a sword shall pierce thy own soul," spoken when the infant was dedicated to God. Now that prophesy had been fulfilled. At that very moment there came to her a sensation not unlike that of cold steel passing through the flesh; the Cross of Christ had pierced her soul.

Beside Mary, and supporting her when she was unable to stand under the pressure of her thoughts and that which her eyes beheld, was John. Of all the disciples, John was the most devoted, the most loving, the most spiritual. One thought permeated every crevice of his heart and mind; the thought that Jesus loved him. He had been with Jesus often during periods of secret communion, the knowledge of which was denied to multitudes of the disciples. But whatever the depth to which his insight may have reached, he was at the moment overcome with but one thought —the departure of his Master. The sharp sword of loneliness pierced him also.

But let us lift our gaze to him who is crucified. He had always found his greatest joy in being servant to others. He had found glory for himself not by seeking his own glory, but by seeking and saving that which was lost. His tears for the sin of the world had not been enough. He must therefore give his life, that he may be worthy to take it again. And being now made perfect through pain, he again finds peace through a sincere concern for Mary, his mother, and John, the disciple whom he loved. The thoughts of Mary are directed away from her own loss. John is to be to her a son, "Woman, behold thy son!" The thoughts of John are directed away from his loss. Mary is to be to him a mother, "Behold thy mother!"

The best balm for pain and sorrow is a duty to be performed; a duty which will consume the energies formerly devoted to brooding over the pain or sorrow. Most of us have probably heard or known of someone who, in the midst of a great loss, devoted himself to some new endeavor with such enthusiasm and interest that the new pursuit was not only successful from the standpoint of man's judgment, but carried with it the personal reward of great joy. The balm should be doubly effective when the new duty, the new pursuit, is one suggested by the Lord of Life. Jesus prescribed well for Mary and John. The prescription for Mary, dictated by the master physician, consisted of the duty to be a mother to John—to bestow her maternal affections on him; to accept his care and concern as from a son. "Woman, behold thy son." With his eyes, for his hands were not free, Jesus must have directed Mary's attention toward the beloved disciple. The prescription for John consisted of the duty to be a son to Mary—to bestow upon her the affections which a son normally has for his mother;

to accept her motherly affection. "And from that hour that disciple took her unto his own home."

By this word from the Cross, our Lord directs our attention to the broken-hearted, to the aged, to home ties, and to loved ones. He would have us carry healing to the broken-hearted, comfort to the aged, reverence to family ties, and good will to all men. It is by no means accidental that the Church has pioneered in the realm of homes for the aged and orphaned, hospitalization and charity. Nor is it mere coincidence that benevolent causes no longer under the supervision of the Church gain their chief support from persons who are a part of the body of Christ. It is all inherent in the Gospel. It is given momentum by a word spoken from the depths of pain and the heights of love: "Woman, behold thy son! . . . Behold thy mother!"

And thus there is established a new relationship among the children of men. Once Jesus had uttered rather startling words—words which may possibly have hurt Mary and his brethren; especially if they were unprepared to appreciate their significance. "For whosoever shall do the will of my Father which is in heaven, the same is my brother, and sister, and mother." All who are obedient to the will of God are members of the family of Christ. It is a family in which love and brotherhood predominate. Earthly ties give way to ties that have their source in heaven. Not that husband or wife, brother or sister, is loved less—but rather that Christ is loved more.

It was not easy for Jesus to break his earthly ties, to place Mary in the same category with all others, but he had a commission from God. In being faithful to that commission, he opened to Mary and John new understanding. That the relationship established between Mary and John at the foot of the Cross did deepen their spiritual insight is borne witness to by the masterly writings on love penned by John at a later date. The brotherhood is our spiritual school. In it we train for the more perfect life. John makes a very blunt statement: "If a man say, I love God, and hateth his brother, he is a liar: for he that loveth not his brother whom he hath seen, how can he love God whom he hath not seen?"

Both Mary and John were obedient to the voice of their Lord—obedient when all that he stood for appeared to be in ruin—and it was given to them to see him come forth victorious. John cared for Mary in his own home until the end of her earthly journey, which probably covered a period of about ten years. He had his reward, even as did Mary. "Verily I say unto you, Inasmuch as ye have done it unto one of the least of these my brethren, ye have done it unto me." There comes to all a duty and a responsibility in the great Kingdom enterprise. And even though truth and righteousness may appear to be on the scaffold, the last word will be spoken by God. "If any man will do his will, he shall know of the doctrine, whether it be of God, or whether I speak of myself." "Woman, behold thy son! . . . Behold thy mother!"

IV. THE FOURTH WORD

"My God, my God, why hast thou forsaken me?" St. Matthew 27:46; St. Mark 15:34.

THIS fourth word, and the three others which follow, were spoken near the end of the period during which our Lord was upon the Cross. It is recorded that darkness covered the land from noon until three o'clock in the afternoon. Just before that period of darkness was broken, and after hours of silence, Jesus musters what physical strength remains, and cries with a loud voice: "My God, my God, why hast thou forsaken me?" It is as though the darkness, combined with the light that was to shine on Easter morning, formed a sacramental background for the word spoken, and for the understanding of the word that would follow. The darkness which gave way to light provided the visible symbol for condemnation giving way to forgiveness; sin giving way to righteousness; death giving way to life. But it is yet dark. The cry is voiced. All who were in the vicinity of the Cross heard. "My God, my God, why hast thou forsaken me?"

The mocking mob, the empty enemies, and the bewildered believers were all represented in the group that heard the cry. The mob snickered, the enemies sneered, and the believers were solemn. The enemies of Jesus felt elated and victorious. They had schemed to have this righteous man put out of the way. He had spoken truth, and they could not stand up under the light of truth. So they used all the tricks they had in their bag to dispose of the Son of God. There had been uncomfortable moments for them; moments when their self-confidence was a bit jarred. It must have made their knees sag a trifle when they heard Pilate publicly proclaim that he found no fault in Jesus. They must have hidden countless fears under their bold front during the early hours of Jesus' stay upon the Cross. Now they felt victorious. The words which came from Jesus suggested to them that he now had given up. He appeared to be making a confession of failure: "My God, my God, why hast thou forsaken me?" And those who loved him—would it not send an alarming chill down their spines? He had never spoken with such words. What could it mean? These were searching moments for that little band who loved him.

There is no reason to doubt that for the moment Jesus actually felt deserted by God—actually felt that God had literally forsaken him and had left him to die uncomforted and alone. It goes almost without saying that Jesus was not one to engage in subtle words. He was not leading his enemies into a trap, so that he could slay them after Easter. He loved his enemies, and prayed for their forgiveness. Nor would he be adding coals to the trials of those who loved him; their trials were already all they could bear. It was from the depth of his soul that he spoke the opening words of the twenty-second Psalm: "My God, my God, why hast thou forsaken me?"

Nor are these words surprising. All the days of life on earth he had lived in intimate fellowship with God. During all those days of temptation and trial and disappointment, his God had never failed him. When it became clear to him that death—his death—on a Cross was the only hope for the world, he did not question the Father's wisdom. He took up the Cross willingly, courageously, and triumphantly. But after all this is said, in view of the inhuman cruelties visited upon him, in view of the abuses endured while on the Cross, the wonder is that he could so long refrain from the utterance which has been puzzling to so many. The end is near at hand. He dips down to the depths of moral perplexity, and pours forth that which he finds there. Thus we today, who do not fully understand the baffling incidents of life, find comfort in the knowledge that our Lord has been there before us.

And although he dipped down to the depths, he did not allow the bond with God in heaven to be severed. He could have said with Job, "Though he slay me, yet will I trust him." He held on. There is no clearer evidence for this fact than the testimony of his own words, "My God, my God." The words are a prayer. God is his God. In this bitterest moment, when he is consuming the dregs, he addresses a communication to his God. "Why hast thou forsaken me?" "Why let me dangle here by such a thin thread?" It was a desperate cry. He sent it forth with a loud voice. "Why? . . . Why? . . . Why?" There is no record of God's answer to the prayer. Only Jesus heard the answer, but we can guess what it must have been. The final word from the Cross provides us with the key. Because Jesus was able to say finally, "Father, into thy hands I commend my spirit," we have every right to suppose that God's answer must have been in this fashion: "Son, I have not forsaken thee. Finish my work."

It remained for those who later experienced the power of the Cross to speak words that would aid our understanding of the cry from the Cross. St. Paul had experienced the power of the Cross. He could write, "For he hath made him to be sin for us, who knew no sin; that we might be made the righteousness of God in him." There had been no sin in his life. Now he is made sin for us men. All the ugliness and filth and blackness of human sin was impressed upon his broken heart. Feeling its weight, and observing its far removal from the things of God, there is little wonder that he should have spoken as he did. One cannot move in the atmosphere of sin without feeling that an awful chasm stands between sin and the Holy Father. Jesus was more spiritually sensitive than any one of us. He had reached higher into the purity of the spirit; he felt more keenly than would any other the decay on which sin thrives. The atmosphere of the Cross appeared for the moment to be far removed from God. Jesus had experienced a portion of the claim made by the Psalmist, "If I ascend up into heaven, thou art there." Now he was experiencing the accompanying claim, "if I make my bed in hell, behold, thou art there." On the faint gleam of light that followed him, Jesus sent up his soul-wrought prayer: "My God, my God, why hast thou forsaken me?" Consciousness of sin is always a symbol of God's being available.

As we today come more and more under the spell of the Cross, we can say with that ancient apostle, "For he hath made him to be sin for us." When we receive the healing forgiveness of his passion, we know that our sin has pierced his heart. We begin to appreciate the burden that forced his cry. "All we like sheep have gone astray; we have turned everyone to his own way; and the Lord hath laid on him the iniquity of us all." He is the scape-goat on whose head is heaped the sins of Christendom. He was sent out into the desert to thirst and die, that we through him might experience in our souls the death of sin; that he might return glorified, and intercede for us, bringing to us the unspeakable joys of eternal life. "My God, my God, why hast thou forsaken me?"

V. THE FIFTH WORD

"I thirst." St. John 19:28.

THE remaining words spoken by our Lord from the Cross follow in rapid succession. His passion is nearly completed. But before announcing the completion of one phase of his Messianic work, and before finally commending his spirit into the hands of God, he utters a statement which by its very nature implies a request. "Jesus knowing that all things were now accomplished, that the scripture might be fulfilled, saith, 'I thirst.' Now there was set a vessel full of vinegar: and they filled a sponge with vinegar, and put it upon hyssop, and put it to his mouth."

In this we have the first direct allusion to his own physical pain. The suffering involved in crucifixion is believed by many to have resolved itself finally into one great pain—the pain of thirst. And if ever any man has doubted that Jesus was true flesh, here is the word that must forever silence such unfounded speculation. "I thirst," he cried. His thirst was real; it was intense. The lips that just a few hours before had reechoed the love and forgiveness which were characteristic of his entire ministry do not hesitate now, all things having been accomplished, to announce in the presence of enemies, scoffers, and soldiers, the great thirst that grips his entire being.

It will be recalled that Jesus had refused the strong wine mixed with drugs offered him earlier. There was in him no desire to have his senses dulled. Although the intentions of the good-hearted women of Jerusalem were probably unselfish and motivated by compassion, Jesus could not accept their dulling potion in the hour when he must be in full command of circumstances. Had he permitted himself to be drugged, he could not have uttered these last words —words by which he opens to earth the windows of his soul. He had gone to the Cross willingly, and he was willing to suffer all the pain that accompanied it. But it was not in Stoic fashion; it was as a hero that he endured. He was not indifferent to pain. He simply bore it courageously. And when all things were accomplished he said, "I thirst," signifying thereby his desire, not for drugs, but for that which ordinarily was satisfying in periods of thirst.

Although the physical thirst which called forth the word appeared on the surface to be something totally beneficial to himself if satisfied, there was that quality about him which made every act of kindness to him beneficial to the person ministering to his need. His every request called forth the good in man. It was so in this case. A hardened, gambling, Roman soldier is touched by the cry. He fills a sponge with vinegar and lifts it by means of a stick of hyssop, to the lips of Jesus. It ought to be noted that the vinegar referred to was not a liquid such as is used today in cookery. It was a light wine in which the alcohol had turned to acetic acid. It was a common and cheap drink carried by the Roman soldiers in much the same fashion as workmen today carry coffee in their lunch pails. Jesus accepted the vinegar. He had called forth the good in a hardened man, and had permitted him to minister to the Son of God in the moment of deepest pain.

We ought also to note that by accepting the vinegar Jesus shows forth a quality of character which we, who are invited to take up our crosses, might well take to heart. It is no easy matter to accept kindness and consideration from one who has brought harm to our person. Often we would rather continue in our pain, however sharp it might be, than accept relief from the hand of him who was in some measure responsible for that pain. But vain pride has no place in the personality of Jesus, and it ought not have any place in the make-up of those who are his disciples. Had the vinegar been given by an apostle or close friend, the whole incident might have passed unnoticed. Jesus accepted the vinegar from one who had nailed him to the Cross, and we pause to consider his God-given strength of character.

To consider only the physical thirst of Jesus would, however, be doing his words a grave injustice. No desire of his, however human it might appear to be, was totally devoid of spiritual content. If Jesus desired refreshment for his body, which he most certainly did, he desired in a fuller measure to bring the world to God. He had a deep spiritual thirst. He thirsted for the souls of men. That thirst was beginning to be quenched when the soldier gave him to drink. And although there is nothing in the gospel narrative to indicate that such was the case, we may well wonder if the soldier who gave him drink was not the same one who later said, "Truly this man was the Son of God." Throughout all the generations that have come and gone since first he announced his great thirst, he has continued to thirst for the hearts and souls of men, that he might take them to himself and present them to God as claimants for the inheritance that fadeth not away. As we today behold him lifted up upon the Cross, not only in history and in mental pictures, but in the life of the world as well, we hear him speak again to us, "I thirst." Will we not hold to his lips the vinegar which his body requires? "Verily I say unto you, Inasmuch as ye have done it unto one of the least of these my brethren, ye have done it unto me."

In bearing patiently the pain of the Cross, and in asking finally for drink, he demonstrates his close kinship with us. Having endured depths of pain such as none of us will ever be called upon to bear, he understands our pains, he feels our human thirst, and he stands beside us as an Elder Brother through whatever we may be called upon to suffer. He knows the close tie between the body and the spirit. He therefore desires that we be not only recipients of whatever healing is available for the body, but also that we be the means through which the distress of others is ministered unto.

As Jesus hangs thirsting upon the Cross, he gives voice to the longings of all who are comfortless and unjustly oppressed. He speaks for the forgotten and those who are passed by. He speaks for the Church as it seeks for those who will do the Lord's work in the local congregation, in the Church at large, and throughout the world. There are those who brand the Church a beggar—our Lord had to beg for enough vinegar that his parched lips might be moistened! Ah, but he who begs moisture for his lips is one who gives to us the water of life. It was he who, standing beside Jacob's well, said to a woman of Samaria, "Give me to drink." And after a brief conversation he adds, "If thou knewest the gift of God, and who it is that saith to thee, Give me to drink; thou wouldest have asked of him, and he would have given thee living water." A few moments later the water of which he speaks is described in this fashion: "But whosoever drinketh of the water that I shall give him shall never thirst; but the water that I shall give him shall be in him a well of water springing up into everlasting life." If the word from the Cross, "I thirst," reminds us of our obligation to Christ, may it also remind us of his willingness to give to us the water of life which, if we drink of it, will satisfy our thirst for eternal life.

VI. THE SIXTH WORD

"It is finished." St. John 19:30.

This brief word of victory and triumph is in some respects akin to Caesar's "Veni, vidi, vici"—I came, I saw, I conquered—in secular literature. Jesus, however, when he came, and seeing the kingdoms of the earth, had no desire to conquer for the purpose of establishing an earthly kingdom. He saw the kingdoms of humanity, and set out to conquer their souls for the Kingdom which is "not of this world." Now the battle is over; the victory is won. It was obviously not the sort of conquest in which every individual was brought into the orbit of the perfect pattern. It was rather like unto the conquest of the physician who has perfected a cure for a particular disease. After the cure has been perfected there yet remains the necessity for those who are diseased to avail themselves of its benefits.

In meditating upon the word, "It is finished," we must be careful to distinguish between "finished" and "ended." A finished work is not necessarily one that is ended, although finishing a work does of necessity bring some things to an end. He who finishes the writing of a great book does not thereby put an end to the book. The labor of organizing the ma-

terials, of writing, and of rewriting are ended. But
the life of the book is just beginning when it is a
finished work. Such would be true of any great labor
of love, whether it be in the field of literature, art,
science, or religion. How much more is it true of
Jesus' labor of love on the Cross! Some things were
ended, but Christ and his Cross were uplifted on a
summit of such height that the influence of him
and his sacrifice could be felt throughout all time.

Jesus had a work to do; a purpose to fulfill; "a
baptism to be baptized with." At the beginning of
his earthly ministry he announced that he had been
anointed to preach the gospel to the poor; to heal
the brokenhearted, to preach deliverance to the cap-
tives, and recovering of sight to the blind, to set at
liberty them that are bruised, to preach the acceptable
year of the Lord. These things had been done, and,
so far as the earthly ministry was concerned, were at
an end. It was his purpose to reveal the Father in
heaven and open to men His Kingdom. This was
done—"he that hath seen me hath seen the Father."
And the revelation stands through all time as the
guide-post for all who would know God.

He had announced unto the twelve, in detail, the
things which must happen—those things which constitute the baptism with which he must be baptized:
"Behold, we go up to Jerusalem, and all things that
are written by the prophets concerning the Son of
man shall be accomplished. For he shall be delivered
unto the Gentiles, and shall be mocked, and spite-

fully entreated, and spitted on: and they shall scourge him, and put him to death: and the third day he shall rise again." He had not, when the sixth word from the Cross was spoken, risen from the dead. Yet it remains true that the work described in the passage just quoted was completed in that the climax—his death—had been reached. The resurrection is implied in the death.

No more must the Son of God walk among men in the flesh, preaching on hillside and by the lake, healing the diseased, enduring in human flesh the abuses of those whose hearts were hard in a cruel age. No more must he be mocked, chastised, spitted upon, nailed to a wooden cross, thirst, and die. These are ended. His earthly career is finished. And like all finished work, the work of our Lord during that period is such that it can stand on its own merits. The plays of Shakespeare, in the world of drama, are a finished work—they stand on their own merit. So it is with the Crucifixion: it is a finished work—it stands on its own merit. Shakespeare wrote over three hundred years ago, but his masterpieces continue to inspire men. Jesus died on the Cross nineteen hundred years ago, and that Cross continues to bring comfort to the children of men, however sore their affliction, however deep their wounds, however grievous their sin.

The bridge between the heart of God and the heart of man was completed. God had never been far distant from man, but man had often remained far distant from God. Man saw but dimly the path he must travel to come into the beauty and holiness of God's presence. Now the bridge is displayed to human observation. We have access to the Father through the Son. The Father makes Himself known to us freely through the Son. This is part of the meaning of the word used by St. John in the prologue of his Gospel—"logos," translated "word" in our Authorized Version. "It is finished." The bridge between God and man is complete and forevermore available for all who would cross the chasm.

Our Lord's work having been finished, although different from the work we are called upon to do, reminds each of us that we have a work to finish. We may truly be called of God to follow some labor, fulfill some purpose in life, or be baptized with some baptism for our own and humanity's benefit, even as our Lord was called of God for a very specialized work. In the course of life we labor, build, endure —may ours at the end be a finished work; a work drawing on the merits of the Cross of Jesus Christ. Then will we be fitted for a place in the Church Triumphant.

VII. THE SEVENTH WORD

"Father, into thy hands I commend my spirit." St. Luke
23:46.

THE last word from the Cross, like the first, is addressed to the Father whom Jesus revealed to earth.
He who knew God intimately, as the only begotten
Son, chose well the words which were to mark his
passing from the body of flesh. They are words of
self-surrender. As such they bring to a fitting climax
the self-less ministry of one fully, and without re-
serve, dedicated to the finishing of God's work.

All human pride and the vain desires of the flesh
were put behind when Jesus showed himself con-
queror of the tempter in the wilderness. During an
earthly ministry which was destined to be brief, he
side-stepped popularity as a physician of the body
when activity in that sphere clashed with his proclaiming the Gospel of God. With firm determina-
tion he marched forth from the retirement and safety
of Caesarea-Philippi to meet the onslaughts of the
enemy. In the garden of Gethsemane he yielded up
the last vestiges of personal desire that God's will
might have complete sway. On the Cross he gave
himself a sacrifice for sin. Surrender of self is written
over every scene. And now, having finished the work

which was his to finish, he reverently commends his spirit into the hands of the Father. "Father, into thy hands I commend my spirit."

As we today stand before the Cross, with hearts tuned to the last word of our dying Saviour, we are reminded of the Christian necessity of self-surrender. "All we like sheep have gone astray; we have turned every one to his own way." The prophet knew human nature. He knew that men give place to personal desires more readily than to the will of God. And Christ, in his risen life, shows us the folly of such misdoings. He bids each one of us allow God first place in our lives, assuring us, through the Holy Spirit, that all things will then work together for our good—yea, for our salvation. The modern idea of self-expression has been good insofar as its application has released ability and capacities, which would otherwise have been repressed, for making life beautiful and for serving humanity. But self-expression can never be a law unto itself, for, if allowed unguided sway, it would bring us death at our own hands. The self that would express goodness, truth and beauty, that would build for life, must surrender to God and allow Him to do and speak through all human creative activities.

There is summed up in this word the essence of how to live and how to die. Commending or committing our spirits into the hands of the Father, our living will be a blessed and joyous experience. He will make us to lie down in green pastures. He will lead us beside the still waters. He will restore our souls. He will lead us in paths of righteousness for his name's sake. He will anoint our heads with oil. Our cups will run over. Goodness and mercy will follow us all our days: and we will dwell in the house of the Lord forever.

And when at last we walk through the valley of the shadow of death, there will be no cause for fear. He will be with us; His rod and staff will comfort us—even as He was with Jesus; and as His rod and staff comforted our Lord. We may at last rest confidently in the kindly hands of the Father, whose arms are everlastingly under and around about His own.

It is said that this seventh word, which is quoted from the Psalms, was the evening prayer of Jewish children. "Into thy hands I commend my spirit." Life, like each day, has its evening and its rest before the dawn. We retire at the evening of each day without fear. There is no doubt in our minds as to the dawning of a new day. It is because of our trust in the laws of nature that we look for the dawning of the new day. How much more ought we trust in the Law of Life, the working of which brings us the assurance of immortality.

PART THREE

IMPORTANT CHRISTIAN BELIEFS

I. THE IMPORTANCE OF BELIEFS

"As a man thinketh in his heart, so is he." Proverbs 23:7.

THESE words may, at first glance, appear to be a strange introduction to the subject of beliefs. But beliefs are related to thinking. They show either the presence or absence of thought. And usually it is the mind rather than the heart which is associated with beliefs. If we can agree that the heart, as here used, is a part of the mind—the subconscious mind, to be more definite—then it becomes clear that the heart is the most important portion of the mind with respect to beliefs. What we think in our hearts makes us what we are.

There is a very obvious distinction between heart and the conscious mind. One may believe in his conscious and reasoning mind that he ought to brush his teeth for the sake of their preservation; that the way of love and forgiveness is the most agreeable manner of conduct; that the Church merits wholehearted support as the essential body of Christianity. These things one may believe, but if they are mere intellectual beliefs, there can be no assurance that the believer will brush his teeth, love and forgive, or support the Church. Heart belief, on the other hand, will always result in a corresponding activity. As one believes in his heart, so he is.

Intellectual belief, unsupported by the heart, is superficial. St. Paul warns against superficial belief when he writes, "Wherefore let him that thinketh he standeth take heed lest he fall." Only the man whose beliefs are deep seated in the heart is in a position to speak of the security of his standing with any degree of certainty.

Of course, it is never easy to convince the heart of something new. Former habits and prejudices and the world of things have "dug in" and have built fortifications and have consolidated their positions. The energized beliefs of Christian quality which we know ought to be in our hearts can be placed there only by sincere effort and desire. Jeremiah has said, "The heart is deceitful above all things, and desperately wicked: who can know it? I the Lord search the heart, I try the reins, even to give every man according to his ways, and according to the fruit of his doings."

The Wise Man has said, "Keep thy heart with all diligence; for out of it are the issues of life." The beliefs stored in our hearts determine our relationships with others; the way in which we conduct our business; the sacrifices we make for the Church and for the extension of the Kingdom; the success of our homes; and the satisfactions of our personal lives. "Man looketh on the outward appearances, but the Lord looketh on the heart." We live under the providence of God, in the final analysis, and not under the dictatorship of man. It is futile to neglect the heart because men see only outward appearances. In the words of the Psalmist, "He (God) knoweth the secrets of the heart."

In considering our Christian beliefs, it should be noted that Christian beliefs are never credulous beliefs. Christian beliefs, when worthy of the name, are supported by a wealth of evidence. Christian beliefs are never indifferent to facts, no matter where those facts have their source. And one of the joys of Protestantism is its freedom to search for truth. Welcome truths are conveyed to us by the senses and by logic, but not held prisoner by them. Then too, Christian beliefs make way for faith. And it often appears that important Christian beliefs were first matters of faith. Jesus once said, "If any man will do his will, he shall know of the doctrine, whether it be of God, or whether I speak of myself." It requires faith to practice the unproved as though it were already certain. And here we touch on an insight to the meaning of St. Paul's words, "Let this mind be in you, which was also in Christ Jesus." Doing the will to know of the doctrine solves the conflict between those who emphasize activity and those who emphasize belief.

One of the favorite verses of those who emphasize the necessity of Christian activity is, "Not every one that saith unto me, Lord, Lord, shall enter into the kingdom of heaven; but he that doeth the will of my Father which is in heaven." It needs to be noted in connection with this verse that the sayings of the conscious mind do not necessarily indicate the beliefs of the heart. Other similar or related verses are these: "Ye shall know them by their fruits." "Inasmuch as ye have done it unto one of the least of these my brethren, ye have done it unto me."

Of the numerous verses emphasizing the importance of belief, we like this one particularly: "He that cometh to God must believe that he is, and that he is a rewarder of them that diligently seek him."

But to argue which is most important, belief or activity, is like arguing which came first, the chicken or the egg. The two march hand in hand. Belief and activity are so bound up with each other that they are inseparable. I submit that there is little possibility of fruitful activity unless activity is backed by worthwhile beliefs of the heart. The reverse would likewise be true—worthwhile beliefs of the heart will show themselves in fruitful activity. "As a man thinketh in his heart, so is he."

Is it important what we believe? Among the groups specializing in the perfecting of diets for the body, there are those who have said that we are what we eat. Undoubtedly there is a large measure of truth in the statement with respect to our physical bodies. In an even larger measure, we are what we believe in our hearts, because we are motivated by our beliefs. We will act upon that which we believe in our hearts. And that upon which we act—even to such a homely matter as brushing our teeth—determines our lives, because God rewards us according to the beliefs upon which we act. The portrayal of the experiences of men and women like ourselves in the pages of Holy Scripture bears witness. To mention but one example, Jairus, who had asked Jesus to heal his daughter, is told that his daughter is dead. Jesus said to him, "Be not afraid, only believe." Jairus believed in his heart. He acted by putting aside fear. He was rewarded according to the belief upon which he acted.

If we are to be blessed of God and receive answer to our prayers, we must first believe: "What things soever ye desire, when ye pray, believe that ye receive them, and ye shall have them." To the penitent person desiring forgiveness for sin, Jesus offers the opportunity for belief. As he was beginning his ministry he said, "Repent ye, and believe the gospel." Among the things counted necessary by devout Christians is the necessity to become sons of God—"As many as received him, to them gave he power to become the sons of God, even to them that believe on his name."

Salvation is likewise bound up with the beliefs of the heart. "Those by the wayside are they that hear; then cometh the devil, and taketh away the word out of their hearts, lest they should believe and be saved." Not all that we hear gets down to the heart. Thus it is that the forces of evil are concerned lest the gospel reach our hearts, and we be saved. "For God so loved the world, that he gave his only begotten Son, that whosoever believeth in him should not perish, but have everlasting life."

Beliefs of the heart are essential to life eternal. "Whosoever liveth and believeth in me shall never die. Believest thou this?" Belief in the gospel is the balm of truth for troubled hearts: "Let not your heart be troubled: ye believe in God, believe also in me." If we take St. John at his word, it was because of his conviction concerning the importance of belief that he wrote his gospel. The whole purpose of the fourth gospel is to inspire belief. "These are written, that ye might believe that Jesus is the Christ, the Son of God; and that believing ye might have life through his name."

Unbelief within the fold of the Church is one of the great hindrances to the advance of God's work. When Jesus was in Nazareth, his ministry was limited by unbelief on the part of those to whom he would have ministered. "And he did not many mighty works there because of their unbelief." There is no reason to doubt that the same principle remains in force among us today.

The chief priests and Pharisees, during the latter portion of Jesus' earthly ministry, knew the power of belief and feared it. "If we let him thus alone, all men will believe on him: and the Romans shall come and take away both our place and our nation." The opportunity to allow the gospel to penetrate to the very depths of our hearts, that we may believe with our whole person, is a powerful tool when appropriated by the Christian.

How important is this matter of belief! It brings

us the assurance or denial of not only personal salvation, but corporate salvation as well. The gates of hell shall not prevail against the Church in this nor any other year, if the hearts of the faithful are bound together by a belief of the gospel. "Be ye all of one mind" (on the essentials of our holy faith).

II. GOD THE FATHER—CREATOR OF ALL

"In the beginning God created the heaven and the earth." Genesis 1:1.

THE opening verse of the Bible states a fundamental belief of the religious man. It is a belief which is filled with greater and more abundant meaning as other portions of the Bible are studied, until finally the Christian is able to say, "I believe in God the Father Almighty, Maker of heaven and earth." This is a tremendous affirmation. In its embrace there is an adequate statement about God. But like all Christian beliefs, it must be believed in the heart to effect a change in us. It is necessary that this affirmation be examined more closely.

Belief in God dates back to the vague beginnings of human history. Unlike early peoples, however, we do not believe in many gods. We go beyond that, and do not admit the existence of other gods. Viewed with a charitable spirit, the gods of the heathen are no more than manifestations of the one true God. Our God is the God of all the universe. How often we meet such phrases as "the Lord he is God: there is none else" in the Scriptures. Jesus, in conversation with one of the scribes, gave the weight of his authority to the declaration, "Hear, O Israel; The Lord our God is one Lord."

The Christian affirmation includes belief in this one God as Creator. He it is who has created heaven and earth and all that is. The Greek philosophers viewed God as creator in the sense of one who builds or moulds from materials already present. They considered the material world evil, and relieved God of responsibility for it. No theory, however, that robs God of his absoluteness, regardless of how many problems it appears to solve, will ever satisfy the heart of him who desires a vision of the truth.

God created the universe and all that is therein. Here the Christian affirmation rightly ends. The Creator is always more powerful than that which he creates. He understands its workings. He knows its strong points and its weak points. He knows its possibilities and its limitations, because there is nothing there that He has not put into it, or allowed to go into it. The Creator is always master of the creation. For this reason the prophets could unhesitatingly proclaim the doom of an evil nation. There was no doubt in their minds as to the fact that the Creator could destroy the creation if He was not pleased with it. Jesus could proclaim that the Kingdom of heaven is at hand because he knew that God would not permit His creation to defeat his purpose.

Is there evidence of creation in this year of our Lord? Or is creation something that happened long ago, was ended, and must be accepted by us on someone else's say-so? Telescopes, which God has permitted man to build for his enlightenment, reveal the fact that beyond the stars which we see in the heavens on a clear night, there are new stars in the process of formation. Creation and re-creation are present facts. Said Jesus, "my Father worketh hitherto." The re-creative works of God are obvious each spring time. On the works of God's re-creation, man must depend. Nor is it true that re-creation continues only in nature. God is not finished with us. In the words of St. John, "it is not yet made manifest what we shall be."

We believe further that this Creator God is Almighty. Because he is Almighty, dependence upon Him dispels all fear from our hearts. He is not only willing, but abundantly able, beyond what we understand, to uphold and govern the heavens and the earth by His eternal providence. The phrase, "providence of God," need not cause any weariness in determining its meaning. It is simply the theological way of saying that nothing comes by chance. In other words, we can depend upon God. His laws cannot be shaken. God never toys with us as a cat toys with a mouse. The laws of nature and of the spirit are His laws, and they never fail. An apple loosed from the tree falls to the ground. And similarly, a soul that is penitent, and that turns to God, experiences forgiveness.

As Christians, we believe that this Creator God, who is Almighty, is also our Father. A father is always a person. And in keeping with the revelation made available through Jesus Christ, we speak of

God as being personal. The word may not be found in the Bible, but the thought is most certainly there. When we read in Genesis of God walking in the garden, it is because the writer thought of Him as a person. This does not mean that our God is anthropomorphic, for Christ tells us that God is a Spirit. Those qualities that set us apart from the rest of creation, that make us persons, are to be found in God—for in His own image He created man. As the Creator of man, He can be no less personal than we are. Where we are concerned, He is a special type of person—a Father. All that an earthly parent is willing to do for the child who is his own flesh and blood, that, and more, God is both willing and able to do for us. The most comforting personal quality of God is stated by St. John in the familiar words, "God is Love." His love for us is so great that often times we suffer, without our understanding why, so that we may be led to depend more fully upon Him. St. Peter exhorts us: "let them that suffer according to the will of God commit the keeping of their souls to him in well doing, as unto a faithful Creator."

This, and whatever else can be said, is not a complete statement about the God in whom we affirm our belief. Moses, it will be remembered, once enquired as to God's name. God replied, "I Am That I Am." God cannot be fully described in terms of anything else. He is always greater than the newest and most complete human knowledge. In the final analysis, God must be defined in terms of Himself. "I

Am That I Am." Said Isaiah, "there is no searching of his understanding."

Of course, the practical question is whether we can find this God. What means are to be used so that we may strengthen the belief of our hearts, remembering that "as a man thinketh in his heart, so is he." The answer can be summed up briefly in private prayer and public worship, and all that these involve. It is doubtful if the neglect of these two can lead to anything other than failure in this realm. Even Jesus our Lord made these the unsung framework of his life and activity. It was his custom to go into the synagogue on the Sabbath. Often he went apart by himself to pray. These are the minimum necessary spiritual exercises.

All worthy beliefs carry with them some benefit. If we believe in "God the Father Almighty, Maker of heaven and earth," we will be different persons than if we did not hold that belief in our hearts. Knowing God as Creator, we will seek to make our wills conform to His will. Knowing that He is Almighty God, we will fear only to do the wrong; have strength and courage to do His bidding, for we will have confidence in His Victory, and share that victory in His Kingdom. Knowing Him as a personal God, we will be enabled to have communion with Him. Knowing Him as Father, we will be able to cast our cares on Him, and will seek the brotherhood of men. Trusting in the providence of God, we will be patient in adversity, knowing that the same may become a blessing. Isaiah sums up the benefits of living under God: "They that wait upon the Lord shall renew their strength; they shall mount up with wings as eagles; they shall run, and not be weary; they shall walk and not faint."

III. JESUS—THE CHRIST OF GOD

"Who say ye that I am? Peter answering said, The Christ of God." St. Luke 9:20.

SOME of the greatest truths can be stated only in the form of paradoxes; statements which seemingly contradict themselves, yet taken together embody truth. It is in this manner that one of the great truths concerning Jesus confronts us. He is like us; and he is unlike us. He is true man; and he is true God. To some psychologists such a statement or analysis would probably indicate a split personality; a malady demanding treatment by a physician of the mind. Christian insight, however, knows the interpretation of such analysis to be not that of split personality, but of the greatest unity known to earth. Jesus is man saturated with God, and totally dedicated to God. Jesus is God expressing Himself as man; God incarnate.

As such, Jesus is the fulfillment of prophetic hope. In him the Law and the Prophets find concrete embodiment. It was the vision and religious knowledge of such a coming reality which filled the life of an ancient patriarch with joy and gladness. "Your father Abraham," said Jesus, "rejoiced to see my day: and he saw it, and was glad." Never has it been sufficient for man simply to rest on the everlasting arms of God, as Creator. Even as Abraham gained strength from beholding that reality which was to come, so we, in a fuller measure, need to fix our gaze firmly upon Jesus, the Christ of God.

Let us look to him, then, as human and as divine. As human he was born a babe in the manger of Bethlehem. He grew through infancy, childhood, youth, to the fullness of manhood. Growth included for him, as it ought for all mankind, an increase in wisdom, stature, and favor with his fellowmen and his God. Occupationally, he toiled at the builder's trade. He was tempted as we are, and because of his sensitiveness to good and evil, faced more penetrating temptations than we can appreciate. He "was in all points tempted like as we are, yet without sin." Knowledge of this fact gives us the assurance that we too have within us the capacity to conquer. To view his life as flesh and blood renews our confidence in the universe, the workshop of God's providence. The universe, under God, produced Jesus, and sustained him. If we will but gaze upon the man Jesus, we will not despair when skies are gray. Anti-Christs appear and attempt to shut off the light, but the universe does not sustain them. Only the Christ-like is given immortal sustenance.

Seen as divine, Jesus is recognized as the Logos, coexistent with God from the beginning. As such, he shows us what God is like; and all who behold the revelation of God in Jesus do not hesitate to say, "God is Christ-like.". "He that hath seen me hath seen the Father." Those who see the seeking love exemplified by Jesus, see in God one of the most comforting aspects of His character. Jesus thus becomes, in a very real sense, the way, the truth, and the life.

For the Christian, Jesus is absolutely essential to the appreciation of God. While it is true that God has not left Himself without witness in any age or any land, no one having tasted of the new wine can be content with the old. Having had the benefit of the true revelation, we can no longer gain complete nourishment from the half-truths of other witnesses. In secular life, a going back to horse-and-buggy days would upset the whole social order. Going back to the pony-express would cause our civilization to collapse. A principle of life is here involved: Man can step upward, but never downward without bringing great loss to himself and others. To step backward in religion is to imperil one's soul.

While it is entirely probable that Jesus does not reveal the totality of God, it is obvious that he reveals all of God that man needs. The sun sends out its rays of light and warmth. All of these rays are not received by earth, yet earth receives all necessary for the continuance of life.

In using the name *Christ,* it is helpful to understand that it means *the anointed.* We, with St. Peter, call Jesus the Christ because, in the words of an ancient creed, "He is ordained of God the Father, and anointed with the Holy Spirit, to be our chief *Prophet and Teacher,* who fully reveals to us the secret counsel and will of God concerning our redemption; and our only *High Priest,* who by the one sacrifice of His body has redeemed us, and ever liveth to make intercession for us with the Father; and our eternal *King,* who governs us by His Word and Spirit, and defends and preserves us in the redemption obtained for us." These three, Prophet and Teacher, High Priest, and King, are termed the offices of Christ.

The multitudes, during Jesus' ministry on earth, recognized him as a prophet and teacher. When he came into Jerusalem on the day of his triumph, the multitude said, in reply to those who inquired about him, "This is Jesus the prophet of Nazareth of Galilee." As an evidence concerning himself, Jesus sent this message to John the Baptist: "The blind receive their sight, and the lame walk, the lepers are cleansed, and the deaf hear, the dead are raised up, and the poor have the gospel preached to them." He differed from lesser prophets and teachers in that he put the seal of his total conduct upon that which he taught.

He became our High Priest chiefly by providing the spotless sacrifice of his own body upon the Cross. In making intercession for the disciples, as he continues to do for those who follow him today, he likewise demonstrated his priestly character. Intercession is a priestly act. After the resurrection, "he lifted up his hands, and blessed them." Allowing himself to be the medium through which a blessing flowed from

God to the assembled group, is likewise evidence of the priestly office which he fills. To the writer of the Epistle to the Hebrews, this priestly office became reason for holding to the Christian profession. "Seeing then that we have a great high priest, that is passed into the heavens, Jesus the Son of God, let us hold fast our profession."

"And he hath on his vesture and on his thigh a name written, King of kings, and Lord of lords." As King, in the realm of the spiritual, he does for man's spirit those things which a good king was normally expected to do in the realm of the national life. He issues to us the law of love, which law must be kept to merit his protection. He protects, and is benevolent to those who give him their allegiance.

A foolish inconsistency may often be observed in the lives of men—an inconsistency of which all of us have been guilty at one time or another. It is this: affirming belief that Jesus is the Christ of God, and denying in practice that his teachings are practical. Too often we behave as though his thought was the unfounded dream of a visionary unsuited for the relationships of our day. It is another instance of the lack of heart-belief.

Although the rewards of believing in the heart that Jesus is the Christ of God are manifold, three resulting benefits should be noted here. One benefit is summed up in that inclusive term, *salvation*. The believer is saved from the burning acids of hate, that he may have joy in love. He is saved from sin, that he

may have forgiveness and new birth. He is saved
from vain pursuits, that he may prepare the way for
the coming of God's Kingdom. He is saved from
death, that he may have true life and immortality.
"Neither is there salvation in any other: for there
is none other name under heaven given among men,
whereby we must be saved."

Another benefit is comprehended in the term *rest*.
"Come unto me, all ye that labor and are heavy laden,
and I will give you rest. Take my yoke upon you, and
learn of me; for I am meek and lowly in heart: and
ye shall find rest unto your souls." Rest, for a healthy
person, and Christ would have us healthy in spirit,
does not consist of the termination of labor and activity and effort. To do absolutely nothing is the most
tiring experience possible to a healthy person. In
pointing out rest as a benefit of belief, we refer to the
rest of purity, strength, and victory.

The benefit of *transformation* carries us far beyond
our present condition, whatever it may be. Jesus
shows us, in his own life, that which we may become.
He assures us finally of a completely victorious transformation, for we shall be like him. To gain these
benefits, we must be convinced in our hearts—another
name for the subconscious—as well as in our minds,
that Jesus is the Christ of God.

IV. THE HOLY SPIRIT—GOD'S ABIDING
PRESENCE

*"And I will pray the Father, and he shall give you
another Comforter, that he may abide with you forever."* St. John 14:16.

ALTHOUGH it is the Holy Spirit who is to abide with
us forever, who is through all ages God's abiding
presence, He is probably the least understood of the
three persons of the Trinity. We speak of God the
Father, and see His Creation around about us. We
speak of His Son, and pictures of Jesus, and things
that Jesus said, come to mind. But oftentimes the
minds of men go blank upon the mention of the Holy
Spirit. Making use of a series of questions should be
helpful in coming to a better understanding of the
Holy Spirit.

From whence does He come? Jesus, speaking of the
Holy Spirit, uses the phrase, "whom the Father will
send in my name." The Father, with whom Christ was
as one, sends Him in Christ's name. His origin is in
the God-head. Theologians have said that He pro-
ceeds from the Father and the Son. But, in another
sense, He has been coeternal God with the Father and
the Son. He was known before the coming of Jesus
Christ. It was by the Spirit, it will be remembered,

that the Prophets spoke the word of God. Through misunderstanding, however, early religious people thought the Holy Spirit available only on special occasions; specifically, when He directed the Prophets and holy men. The Psalmist seems to have been conscious of the Holy Spirit's dwelling in him, for he prays, "take not thy Holy Spirit from me." Joel, with advancing vision, foresees the day when God will pour out his Spirit upon all flesh. Jesus, finally, assures us of the reality of the prophet's vision—"And I will pray the Father, and he shall give you another Comforter, that he may abide with you forever."

But who is the Holy Spirit? What understandable terms may we use to describe Him, at least partially? (1) He is God in action, working through men, achieving God's purposes in history. He it is who has led men to a better understanding of, and appreciation for, God; who is advancing the advent of God's Kingdom on earth. Although a short view of history seemingly contradicts this thought, a long and inclusive view will leave the observer impressed with the forward strides which have been made.

(2) He is the pulse that beats between God and man, bringing and renewing life in man. As the blood in the human body flows through all parts of the body, carrying off waste, bringing nourishment, and sustaining life; so the Holy Spirit touches the life of the world, carrying off waste, bringing nourishment, sustaining true life. Sometimes the world becomes sick, as does the human body on occasion. At such

times poisons are secreted into the stream of life in greater quantity than is the case under more normal conditions. At such times the healing process is prolonged according to the magnitude of the disease. The world today is sick as a result of its having neglected the true God, but the life of God is available to the world through the Holy Spirit.

(3) He is God dwelling within each of us individually. There is a spark of God within each of us. It is that spark which kindles the pure and holy life; that makes possible our deeds of love and mercy; that through us speaks wisdom and understanding, counsel and might, knowledge and the fear of the Lord.

(4) He is God drawing men together in the fellowship of the Kingdom. In the Church, there is a tie that binds those of like mind into one holy fellowship; which permits us, who have come out of different backgrounds and experiences, to worship and serve as one. That bond is strengthened or weakened according as the Holy Spirit is permitted, by us, to reign. The world, the gates of hell, lose power in proportion as self is forgotten in loving service to God and as the Spirit of God is let free to reign. The Holy Spirit moves in proportion to the opportunity afforded by man. Does this not explain the miracle of Pentecost? They were all together in one place, offering no resistance whatsoever, and the Spirit was poured out upon them abundantly.

(5) He is God speaking to us through inspired

writings and proclamations. Individual writers and messengers become channels through which the Holy Spirit may work on a larger basis than that of the individual, for the enlightenment of multitudes.

What is our relationship to Him? God is Father. On occasion we speak of the Son as our Elder Brother. In St. John's Gospel, the Holy Spirit is described as an advocate whose work must lead to a conviction. His presence among us leads to our being convicted of either sin or righteousness. Closing him out of our lives is the sin without forgiveness, according to the Gospel. And this is easily understood, for if he is the pulse that beats between God and man, to close Him out is to close the way to God, making it impossible to ask forgiveness, and for God to grant the same.

What are the benefits of belief in the Holy Spirit; of allowing Him to dwell within us? (1) Such belief helps us in our prayer life. In a given instance, we may feel that we do not know how to ask aright. The Spirit will help us in such infirmities: "The Spirit also helpeth our infirmities: for we know not what we should pray for as we ought: but the Spirit itself maketh intercession for us with groanings which cannot be uttered." Communion with God is a benefit of great magnitude.

(2) Such belief provides inner strength. St. Paul speaks of being "strengthened with might by his Spirit in the inner man." The first and primary strength needed by anyone is strength to rule himself—to control his own life. Only thus can we hope to make a

worthy impression on the world. Only by laying a firm foundation within ourselves can we hope to inherit abundant life. The Spirit will grant strength. Most of us could trace a large portion of our weakness to neglect of the Holy Spirit.

(3) Such belief makes rebirth possible. As we are given life in the world of flesh, and we understand it not, so also may we receive life in the world of spirit by the working of the Holy Spirit within us. "Except a man be born of water and of the Spirit, he cannot enter into the kingdom of God. That which is born of the flesh is flesh; and that which is born of the Spirit is spirit." The blowing of the wind was a mystery to Nicodemus, and Jesus spoke of rebirth as a similar mystery. It is mystery, but fact—essential fact.

(4) Such belief encourages transformation. St. Paul speaks of the "renewing of the Holy Spirit." The old man of lovelessness is put off and we are transformed into persons capable of loving God and our fellowmen. This transformation is a benefit of the Holy Spirit. To be led by the Holy Spirit permits our being not simply creatures, but sons. "For as many as are led by the Spirit of God, these are the sons of God."

(5) Such belief provides us with power to be Christ's witnesses. "But ye shall receive power, after that the Holy Spirit is come upon you: and ye shall be witnesses unto me both in Jerusalem, and in all Judea, and in Samaria, and unto the uttermost part of the earth."

(6) Such belief makes possible our having the guidance so sorely needed in the maze of current life. "He shall teach you all things, and bring all things to your remembrance, whatsoever I have said unto you."

V. THE FORGIVENESS OF SINS

"If we say that we have no sin, we deceive ourselves, and the truth is not in us. If we confess our sins, he is faithful and righteous to forgive us our sins, and to cleanse us from all unrighteousness." I John 1:8, 9.

WE cannot hope for an appreciative understanding of the forgiveness of sins unless there is first an understanding of the nature of sin. Many definitions, each providing some light, have been proposed. But briefly, sin embraces all that separates man from man, and that separates man from God. As such it includes disobedience to the law of God, which law requires that we love God with our whole being, and our neighbor as ourselves. Sin, from the standpoint of the law of love, becomes lovelessness. Any activity intended to bring harm to the least among men; or any good that could have been done for the least among men and was not done, is, in the final analysis, sin against God. "Inasmuch as ye did it not to one of the least of these, ye did it not to me." The Psalmist cried, "Against thee, thee only, have I sinned."

Because sin is of such nature, none escapes the guilt of sin. St. Paul gives us the matter-of-fact statement: "For all have sinned, and come short of the glory of God." We have added daily to our guilt. We have not been perfect, as our Father in heaven is perfect. We have closed the door upon many opportunities to grow in Christ-likeness. Our particular cross has not been borne daily in the spirit of Jesus. "All we like sheep have gone astray; we have turned every one to his own way." "If we say that we have no sin, we deceive ourselves, and the truth is not in us."

But God is faithful. He does not permit the curse of sin to hang heavily upon us without also opening to us a way of release. He is willing to open to us the rivers of forgiveness. He will allow them to flow through us, washing us until we are whiter than snow. "If we confess our sins, he is faithful and righteous to forgive us our sins, and to cleanse us from all unrighteousness." St. John seemingly comprehends a number of things in the simple word, confess. It is clear from other Scriptures that the admission of sin is not in itself sufficient to receive forgiveness. Although the admission or confession of sin is the first and essential step, it must be followed by repentance, which includes sorrow for sin and the honest intention to amend our ways. It is after repentance, and all that it involves, that forgiveness is found. Jesus, at the beginning of his ministry, gave the timeless exhortation, "Repent ye, and believe the gospel." Forgiveness is one of the chief promises of the gospel, and it follows naturally from the fact that God is Love. No sin, however great, is beyond the bounds of possible forgiveness.

The nature of forgiveness is usually more puzzling

than a general admission of its reality. Forgiveness does not mean that law is brushed aside. Never does it mean that a man can sow tares, and, through forgiveness, reap wheat. The law of the harvest remains intact—"Whatsoever a man soweth that shall he also reap." The forgiven man sees punishment as disciplinary and does not become bitter. As it has been said, the sinner has a right to his punishment. Although forgiveness does not set aside any moral law or any law of nature, it does bring into power, in the forgiven man, a higher law which makes possible the healing of the consequences of sin. Peter, at the palace of Annas, sinned when he denied that he knew Jesus. "And the Lord turned, and looked upon Peter." "And Peter went out, and wept bitterly." Peter suffered the consequence of his sin. But forgiveness brought healing, and strengthened him, and made it possible for him to be a chief witness of Jesus, bold to proclaim truth. Very often we suffer first, not according to justice, but according to mercy. Of course, we dare not expect such. To sin with the expectation of escaping punishment through forgiveness makes forgiveness very difficult. The false doctrine of such forgiveness was one of the causes leading to the Reformation.

When one experiences forgiveness, he feels, while suffering the penalty, that God has not forsaken him, but is seeking him. This may be illustrated with an incident from the life of David. After David had sinned with Bathsheba, and had permitted Uriah, her husband, to be smitten and die, he confessed to the prophet Nathan, "I have sinned against the Lord." And Nathan said unto David, "The Lord also hath put away thy sin; thou shalt not die. Howbeit, because by this deed thou hast given great occasion to the enemies of the Lord to blaspheme, the child also that is born unto thee shall surely die." Although forgiven, David knew he must bear the coming punishment. He knew that in the punishment God was seeking him, and healing him, and fortifying him against sinning in that manner again.

Forgiveness is a transaction in which both God and man have their respective functions to perform. Consider the parable of the prodigal son. There the son suffered as a result of his own sin. But is it not also clear that the father, representing God, also suffered because of the son's sin? The son admitted his sin, and was sorry for it, and determined to mend his ways. Then, and then only, was the father able to show compassion, and restore the son to the home. God gives of Himself, when He forgives, by identifying Himself with the sinner. This was done most vividly on Calvary. How familiar are the words, "God so loved . . . that he gave."

"Unto whomsoever much is given, of him shall be much required." This applies in the matter of forgiveness. He whose sins are forgiven by God must forgive those who wrong him. We recall the parable of the servant who had been forgiven a tremendous debt by the king. But having been forgiven, he went out and laid hands on a fellow servant who owed him an insignificant amount. His unwillingness to forgive the fellow-servant made of non-effect the forgiveness received from the king. At the end he was made to suffer the full penalty for his debt. If we would ourselves seek forgiveness, we must remember the Gospel exhortation: "And when ye stand praying, forgive, if ye have ought against any: that your Father also which is in heaven may forgive you your trespasses."

Some will say, Is it not through Christ that we have forgiveness of sins? So we believe, and so we teach. But we must also remember that there was forgiveness of sins before the Cross of history. Some of the most beautiful thoughts on forgiveness come to us from the Old Testament. Says the Psalmist, "For thou, Lord, art good, and ready to forgive; and plenteous in mercy unto all them that call upon thee." Again, "As far as the east is from the west, so far hath he removed our transgressions from us." The prophet Isaiah writes, "Though your sins be as scarlet, they shall be as white as snow; though they be red like crimson, they shall be as wool."

These in no way contradict St. John's statement that "the blood of Jesus Christ his Son cleanses us from all sin." Christ mediates forgiveness to us in the sense that through his perfect sacrifice on the Cross, he brings God much nearer to man than He ever was before. By his being lifted up, God's forgiveness became more understandable, and available in fuller measure to all the world.

Yet after all is said that can be said, forgiveness must be experienced as well as theorized about. It is a fact by which man can live, however he explains it. The reward for belief in the forgiveness of sins, is the forgiveness of sins.

VI. THE CHURCH—CHRIST'S BODY

" (God) gave him to be the head over all things to the church, which is his body, the fulness of him that filleth all in all." Ephesians 1:22, 23.

IT is clear, on a basis of the text, that the Church is not simply one of many human organizations. Rather, it is the body of Christ, of which he is the ever living head. In much the same manner as we are the heads of our bodies, directing their parts and movements, permeating them throughout, so Christ directs the Church, his body, and fills it with his fullness. Seen as the body of Christ, the Church is the continuation of Jesus' earthly life and ministry. St. Mark very significantly begins his Gospel, "The beginning of the gospel of Jesus Christ, the Son of God," assuring us that that which was in Jesus, while in the flesh, was but the beginning of that which continues in the Church. St. Luke, in his Acts of the Apostles, referring to his Gospel, says, "The former treatise have I made, O Theophilus, of all that Jesus began both to do and teach." Here again there is emphasis on the fact that Jesus' earthly ministry was but the beginning. The Church is the continuation of his life and work. As the body of Christ, the

Church goes into the world with credentials bearing the seal of God—"As my Father hath sent me, even so send I you."

Upon the mention of the word *Church,* a number of different things may come to our minds. Perhaps we will think of our own particular denomination as such. Again, we may think of the local Church, either as a congregation—the sum total of the membership—or as the building in which the congregation worships. What we do not always remember is that these are but parts or members of the total body of Christ, and, on the other hand, that these parts are manifestations of the fullness of Christ. The presence of the Church is the assurance of Christ's presence; and our membership in the Church, if we are faithful to the vocation wherein we are called, is our assurance that we are members of Christ.

Jesus Christ is both the founder and the foundation of the Church. St. Peter said of Jesus, "Thou art the Christ, the Son of the living God." Then said Jesus, "upon this rock I will build my church; and the gates of hell shall not prevail against it." Jesus clearly states that he is the founder, the builder of the Church. Such being the case, the Church is not of human origin. When men and women are called into membership in the Church, it is, in the final analysis, God calling them into His Kingdom. Christ is the creator and the sustainer of the Church. And he has made himself the foundation of the Church. "Upon this rock," referring to the statement of his sonship and divinity, "I will build my church." How beautifully the hymn writer has stated this truth:

> "The Church's one foundation
> Is Jesus Christ her Lord;
> She is His new creation
> By water and the word:
> From heaven He came and sought her
> To be His holy bride;
> With His own blood He bought her,
> And for her life He died."

Obviously, Christ has a two-fold claim upon the Church from its earliest beginnings. It is his by virtue of creation. That which one creates is normally supposed to be the possession of the creator. In creating the Church, Christ used those persons who were given to him by the Father. The Church is also his by virtue of his having purchased it on Calvary's Cross. "Christ also loved the church and gave himself for it."

Within recent generations there has seemingly grown up the idea that one can be a Christian outside the Church. This is a man-made doctrine without Scriptural foundation. Often it is resorted to to cover some greater love than the love of Christ— some may even believe it. The New Testament knows nothing of Christians apart from the Church or brotherhood.

The promises of the Gospel are to individuals. That is true. It is also true, and probably more correct, to say that the promises of the Gospel are to the Church. Surely no one would deny that the promises of Christ are, for each of us, dependent upon obedience to his commands. It requires very little study to see that one cannot be obedient to his commands apart from the Church. Consider the command, "Go ye therefore, and teach all nations, baptizing them in the name of the Father, and of the Son, and of the Holy Ghost." No one could possibly begin to obey that command apart from the Church, through which, by the total gifts of the members, the command is obeyed. When Christ instituted the Holy Communion, he said, "this do in remembrance of me." The Church is the only agency on earth authorized to give the sacred elements to its members.

To believe in the Church with one's whole heart is to be a member of the Church, interested in its activities, supporting its endeavors with time, talent, and possessions, and seeking to win others to Christ. Such conduct is not without its fitting reward.

To be an integral part of the Church is to be bound closer to Christ than would otherwise be possible. We show our love for that which he loved. We mingle with those whom he loves. This mingling of our affections with his must eventually draw us nearer to oneness with him.

Being a part of the Church, through active membership in it, makes our efforts count for something. Although we are constantly being reminded that the world is small, there is a very real sense, so far as individuals are concerned, in which the world is large —very large. Individual effort, unless one insists on pointing to a half dozen exceptional men, is lost when not combined with the efforts of other like-minded persons.

The Church aids in our seeking to be obedient to Christ. Not only does it make obedience possible to such commands as have been mentioned, missions and communion, but it makes all easier and more probable of fulfillment. The Church member has the united support of the entire Church in seeking to do Christ's will.

The Church is a source of inspiration to each of its communicants. By the beauties of fellowship, music, and worshipping together in an holy atmosphere, each is lifted above himself. If we, as individuals, permit the truths and beauties that come to us through the Church to become a part of ourselves, we will never again be satisfied with life outside the fold. To be uplifted by the inspiration of the Church, is to grow heavenward.

The Church may become for us a means of salvation. Of course, no human can honestly assure every Church member of salvation. On the other hand, every person who sincerely desires salvation will not hesitate to seek the Church. A traveler desiring to cross the ocean would not risk the perils of a rowboat. He would take the large ocean liner. There he would feel relatively secure. In a somewhat similar manner, there is a greater degree of security in following the beaten pathway of the Church.

The Church Militant provides a suitable preparation for the Church Triumphant. Participation in the life of the Church is not always a bed of roses. It involves sacrifice and, on occasion, suffering. But this is in reality an argument for the Church, for it is this fact which permits us to share the sufferings of Christ, whereby only dare we hope for the crown of life.

VII. THE LIFE EVERLASTING

"If a man die, shall he live again?" Job 14:4.

THE question voiced by Job is the question of the ages. Each generation asks, and each generation ends by answering in the affirmative. Belief in the life everlasting is universal among men, except for an occasional perverted mind. Jesus did not argue about immortality. He knew life beyond the grave as an accepted fact under God, and never doubted. He taught and lived on the basis of the certainty of everlasting life. That is important. Living as though our end was to be like unto that of the grass of the field is not the proper atmosphere for a meaningful conviction. If we would believe in immortality, we must live as though we were immortal.

Although the belief in immortality is universal, the Christian has the surest basis for his belief. Our Lord himself demonstrates to the disciples the truth and reality of the belief. By his life and resurrection, he brought immortality out into the open. With St. Paul, every Christian can speak of "our Saviour Jesus Christ, who hath abolished death, and brought life and immortality to light through the gospel." To behold the risen and living Christ is to put aside for all time the pagan fear of the grave. To know Christ

as having already entered the portals of the life everlasting is to accept the certain hope of immortality
joyfully.

Naturally we are inclined to ask how Christ's pos-
sessing the life everlasting affects us. Is there any
relation between his ascending to the Father and the
hope to which we hold? This is certain: The God who
would not permit Jesus to be held a captive by the
grave is also our God. "I ascend unto my Father, and
your Father; and to my God, and your God."

Each of us, as individuals, is given the opportunity
to lay hold on everlasting life because our God is
one who values each of us individually. The insight
that God values the individual human personality is
one of the distinctive characteristics of the Christian
religion. Nowhere else in the history of thought does
this fact stand out so vividly. "The very hairs of your
head are all numbered." It would be unreasonable to
even suppose that God would permit that life to be
snuffed-out for which so much concern was given.

In speaking of the life everlasting, our thoughts,
as Christians, turn naturally toward heaven. Heaven
has become the accepted term for the place where the
life of the righteous continues beyond the veil of
this earthly life. While we may on occasion draw
upon earthly figures of speech to suggest the splendor
of heaven, it must finally be realized that heaven
cannot be adequately described in terms of the things
known on earth. "Eye hath not seen, nor ear heard,
neither have entered into the heart of man, the things

which God hath prepared for them that love him."

There are in the Scriptures, however, glimpses of the nature of the life everlasting. St. Paul tells us that this body of flesh will give way to a spiritual body. "It is sown a natural body, it is raised a spiritual body. There is a natural body, and there is a spiritual body." Just what a spiritual body is is a question beyond answering in the terms of earth. This much seems clear: It will be a better body than the physical. Many of us would not want to look forward to continuing forever in our present bodies. These physical bodies are subject to disease; they become bruised; they cause us various undesirable concerns. Hereafter we shall have spiritual bodies.

Life, viewed in its totality, is not dependent upon the physical body. The physical body is simply one manifestation of the individual personality. Christ assures us that the soul is stronger than the flesh in the exhortation: "Fear not them which kill the body, but are not able to kill the soul." It was this thought which brought comfort to Zwingli, one of the Reformation fathers, during his dying moments on the battlefield. His final words were, "What evil is there in this? They are able, it is true, to kill the body but not the soul."

St. Paul illustrates the rising of the spiritual body by referring to the planting of grain. "And that which thou sowest, thou sowest not that body that shall be, but bare grain, it may chance of wheat, or of some other grain: but God giveth it a body as it hath pleased him, and to every seed his own body." Each receives its own body, but not the same body. So it is with us. In the life everlasting each shall receive his own body, but not the same body here possessed. Scientists tell us that we receive a new body of flesh every seven years. The cells of our flesh die and are passed off as waste. New cells take their place. Yet with this never ending change, we do not lose our individual characteristics. Knowledge of this physical fact makes it easier for us to comprehend the fact that we shall have different bodies hereafter. There will be provided for us spiritual bodies. In these spiritual bodies we will recognize and know each other.

In the life everlasting, the Christian will have the feeling of being at home. There will be no strangeness for those who have lived in fellowship with Christ. Each will be at ease and enjoy the blessing of a home-like freedom. Jesus' statement, "In my Father's house are many mansions," brings us the simple assurance that heaven is home for all to whom God is Father.

The life everlasting will provide us with the opportunity to carry on from where activity ceased on earth. When one is very tired from some strenuous activity, he may be inclined to hope for a heaven of inactivity. A sufficient period of inactivity would convince anyone, however, that such is not to be desired. Enlarged opportunities and responsibilities would seem to be suggested by the statement, "Well done, thou good and faithful servant: thou hast been faithful over a few things, I will make thee ruler over many things; enter thou into the joy of thy lord."

Who, then, shall inherit this everlasting life? There are a number of Scriptural passages which at least point the way to an answer. Those who hear the word of Christ and believe in God have everlasting life. "He that heareth my word, and believeth on him that sent me, hath everlasting life." Having had the opportunity to come to a knowledge of Christ, the person who accepts God with a believing heart is well on his way to his eternal home. In much the same manner, there is the statement, "He that believeth on the Son hath everlasting life." Belief, it needs to be remembered, is not simply a matter of mental accent, but also of heart conviction.

Those who permit no earthly possession or human tie to stand between them and Christ shall inherit everlasting life. "And every one that hath forsaken houses, or brethren, or sisters, or father, or mother, or wife, or children, or lands, for my name's sake, shall receive an hundred-fold, and shall inherit everlasting life." The familiar incident of the rich young ruler is a case in point of one who permitted earthly possessions to stand between him and Christ. Even such honored bonds as family ties should not be permitted to stand between a man and Christ. All persons who keep the lines of communion with Christ open, have, to their benefit, the available channels for receiving that nourishment which will sustain them unto life eternal.

The whole matter may well be summed up by saying that the best insurance for everlasting life is a worthy conviction which permeates the whole of life. It is a matter of living worthy of the Kingdom in thought and act. "He that soweth to the Spirit shall of the Spirit reap life everlasting," says St. Paul.

PART FOUR

THE INCLUSIVE PRAYER

I. THE IMPORTANCE OF PRAYER

"After this manner therefore pray ye." St. Matthew 6:9.

THIS phrase will be recognized as introductory to the Lord's Prayer as it is recorded in the Gospel according to St. Matthew. Prayer is an essential of true religion. Without prayer religion becomes very shallow. Indeed, without it religion would probably pass out of existence. Jesus gave no elaborate instructions relative to prayer, or at least none have been preserved for us. But he definitely did that which is of far greater significance. He showed us in his humanity the power of a life which is nourished by prayerful communion with God. He himself prayed. And he taught his disciples a prayer which was both simple and yet more inclusive than any prayer known to man. We call it the Lord's Prayer. The chapters which follow are concerned with the study of the various parts of that prayer.

But first we need to pause and consider some of the reasons why prayer is important. Our Christian faith has, through the gift of God, preserved to each of us a measure of freedom; has enabled us to assert a degree of personal independence. This possession has become very precious to us. We glory in the priesthood of believers. Yet we need merely

glance at secular life to see how dependent independence really makes us. He who is considered in-
dependent is dependent upon the stability of the
monetary system, the industry of those who make
investments profitable, and the honesty of those who
serve. Our Christian freedom and independence
make us dependent upon God. He who denies his dependence upon God, and refuses to accept the spiritual benefits of God through the channel of prayer,
denies himself the benefits of spiritual freedom made
available through Christ, and sins against the Holy
Ghost.

It appears that there are two major reasons why
prayer is important. Prayer is important because God
desires it. As a king desires homage, so God desires
our prayers; as a righteous judge listens to the testimony of each, so our God hears our prayers; yea, as a
father longs for fellowship with his children, God
longs for communion with His children. And we will
notice, as we study the Lord's Prayer, that it is God-
centered throughout except for the request for bread
—and we cannot be entirely sure that physical bread
is here intended.

Prayer is important not only because God desires
it, but also because man needs it. This is probably
of more immediate concern to us. If we come to a
realization that prayer is necessary for us, then prayer
becomes an issue of paramount importance. A glance
at the life of Jesus is suggestive. Usually we freely
admit that he was the Son of the Most High God.

Because such was his nature, we attribute to him much that is beyond us in wisdom and in power. If ever there was a person whose independence was free from dependence, he was that person. Yet we find him going apart often to pray. He rose up early in the morning to pray, valuing prayer above sleep. Without prayer, he was not prepared for the emergencies of the day. How much more is prayer essential to each one of us! A noble deed, a clean life, is not the best prayer as some would contend. Instead, it is prayer that makes these effective. Prayers consist of spoken words. The introduction to the Lord's Prayer in the Gospel according to St. Luke reads, "When ye pray, *say* . . ." Prayers are words, not deeds. But prayers are not simply words. They are first quiet meditation. And after spoken, they are the expectant listening for a reply.

Stillness such as prayer involves is a needed corrective for the rush and compulsion of present day living. The rush, rush, rush, with this obligation and that; the 'come here' and 'go there' invitations of a complex society; the fears and anxieties that seemingly are too common to man, will wear heavily on the strongest man unless there is some corrective. Prayer is such a corrective, bringing peace and unity to life. The peace of mind possessed by Mahatma Gandhi has been a source of wonder to many, but it is no secret. Here is what he says, "Prayer has saved my life. Without it I should have been a lunatic long ago."

Prayer is the only avenue open to man by which he may establish a personal relationship with God. Nothing less than a personal relationship with God can satisfy the cold fact of our insufficiency. It is in the prayer chamber that the words from Zechariah take on significance. "They shall call on my name, and I will hear them: I will say, It is my people: and they shall say, The Lord is my God." This is the warmth that the chill of life demands. We are His people. He is our God. It comes as a result of prayer.

After having established a personal relationship with God through prayer, we are enabled to be obedient to Him. We are unable to love our fellow-men as we ought—these whom we have seen—how much less can we love God whom we have not seen, unless we are granted the capacity to obey. The Beatitudes hold forth so many attractive blessings, but they seem so far-off and unreal. Indeed, they must remain far-off and unreal unless we grow in spirit and in character. Such growth is possible only if we have the capacity to obey gained through prayer.

Prayer is the nourishment for Christian growth. It nourishes the creature of God to the point where he becomes a son of God. It is for a purpose, namely, of becoming sons of God, that we are created. There is every reason why we should be ill at ease so long as we are not moving in that direction. Augustine has said, "Thou hast made us for Thyself, and our hearts are restless until they repose in Thee." Man, to have life, must be in a continual state of becoming. And man becomes more and more like that from which he gains nourishment for the life he is living. Those who hold communion with the powers of evil move further and further away from God and His promises. Those who pause at regular intervals for prayer with the living God become more and more God-like. Prayer is essential for all who believe that Jesus meant what he said when he uttered the exhortation, "Be ye therefore perfect, even as your Father which is in heaven is perfect." Some will say, How can we ever be perfect, being now so imperfect and sinful? Jesus said, "Except a man be born again, he cannot see the kingdom of God." Perhaps growth is too often thought of as simply becoming more of what we already are. Let us look to the fruit trees. As the blossom grows, it does not become a larger blossom. It grows into something entirely different, the fruit. So with us, growth means change into something better. Prayer changes him who prays by supplying the nourishment of true growth. Let him who is content simply to become more of what he already is beware and pray not. Prayer changes us.

While the praying man is being thus transformed, there comes to him an increased and increasing knowledge of God's purposes. God knows better than we ourselves know what things we have need of. He who has made progress in the prayer life does not attempt to change God's mind. Rather, he desires that his heart and will and mind be receptive to the plans of God; that he be enabled further to harmonize his actions with God's divine plan. Such increased harmonization with the purposes of God will mean increased identification with God. In Jesus, our Lord, we have the one example of perfect identification with the purposes of God. "I and the Father are one."

To pray with an increased understanding of God's purposes is to be empowered to do such good works as are pleasing in His sight; to gain the privilege of having our diseases healed and the storms of life calmed; to have God act in us and through us and for us.

There come times in the lives of us all when the need of prayer is felt keenly. Nothing known on earth satisfies. Only the breath of heaven could possibly help. The present is the time to lay the foundation for the structure which the future need will demand. "Seek ye the Lord while he may be found, call ye upon him while he is near: let the wicked forsake his way, and the unrighteous man his thoughts: and let him return unto the Lord, and he will have mercy upon him; and to our God, for he will abundantly pardon."

Modern labor has become a monotone, for the most part. There are but few, comparatively speaking, whose work is creative. All of us need divine inspiration to carry on, regardless of where we are or what we are. None of us have within ourselves the resources to carry on joyfully, much less the resources from which to gain eternal satisfaction from the menial duties with which we are confronted. God is the only solution. The God who hears prayer grants peace such as the world can neither give nor take away.

II. BEGINNING TO PRAY

"Our Father which art in heaven." St. Matthew 6:9.

ALL prayer that is worthy of the name begins with a firm belief in God. As the author of the epistle to the Hebrews clearly states, "he that cometh to God must believe that he is, and that he is a rewarder of them that diligently seek him." This truth appears so obvious as to make mention of it seemingly unnecessary. Yet how often we have repeated prayers together in public worship, especially the Lord's Prayer, without giving conscious recognition to the fact that God is, that He hears prayer, and that He does reward all who diligently seek to have communion with Him. Without the conviction that God is not only real, but is in Himself complete Reality; that God is a true person, having the capacity to receive and dispatch communications—we will find ourselves without a vital prayer experience. We are familiar with the importance of prayer, but we cannot have for ourselves the benefits of prayer unless we believe in our hearts that God is. The God at the end of a logical argument for His existence; the God whom others tell us exists; the God whose word we read in sacred writings, can avail us little unless in our hearts there is a conviction of His being that transcends all arguments and hear-say, pleasing as these may be to the mind.

But the prayer of him who believes that God is, is further determined by his conception of God. It is not enough to believe that God is. We must have at least a glimpse of what God is like. If He is a ruthless tyrant, we must pray as slaves to a deaf ear. If He is a Father, as Jesus showed Him to be, we may use the petitions of the Lord's Prayer, making them our own, and may add, in our secret chambers, such other communications as may be addressed to One who is willing and able to hear the Lord's Prayer.

Jesus, in his prayers, addressed God as "Father." "Father" must have been the most truly descriptive and the most adequate name in the vocabulary of man, else Jesus would not have used it. He bids us address God as "Father," for he knew that if we were to pray as we ought, and receive thereby the rewards of rightly directed and diligent prayer, we must first have a true conception of God.

"Father" is a distinctly Christian name for God. And although the name may have been used on occasion by members of the Jewish nation prior to the advent of Jesus, the name as there used did not rise much above the thought that God was Father of Israel alone. This was a very narrow conception, and unworthy of Him who is the creator of the ends of the earth. The Christian use of the name is also narrow, as we shall see later, but it is a narrowness that liberates, in that it permits the Chinaman to re-

main a Chinaman, the Englishman to remain an
Englishman, the American to remain an American,
and yet be a member of a transcending brotherhood
under one Father in heaven.

"Father" is a name full of meaning. It is a the-
ology in miniature. It conveys to us the truth about
God, the truth about ourselves, and the truth about
others. As the truth about God, we are shown One
who has the qualities of the best human father conceivable, elevated above the weaknesses of human
flesh, and having all power and all dominion in
heaven and on earth. Too often we have thought
of the Father in heaven as being Love, and have
been content to give His fatherly love rather loose
interpretation. God *is* Love. Let us be sure of that;
for if He is not Love there is no point to our praying.
It is in the interpretation of Love that many have
stumbled. God, as Father, loves us so much that for
our own good He cannot grant some of our requests.
He must say "no" to our foolish desires. He loves us
so much that He must punish us when we disobey,
else how would we, frail men, learn the joy of
obedience.

God is our Father; we are His children. That is
the truth about us. We are called sons of God. It
makes all the difference in the world whether we look
upon ourselves as simians—ape-like animals—or
whether we know ourselves to be sons of the Most
High. It makes all the difference in the world whether
we believe ourselves to be the creation of blind ma-

terial force, in which case death would end all, or whether we know ourselves to be the creation of a loving heavenly Father, and having within ourselves the seed of immortality. What we believe about ourselves in these respects will determine our motives and our habits, our work and our play; in short, it will be the dominant note in our lives, sounding in and above all that we think or say or do. Knowing ourselves to be related to God as a son is to his father, our prayers will reflect our favored position, and our petitions will be for such graces and things as are proper for a child of God.

If God is our Father, and we are His sons, then it is clear that we are brethren. Now there is, generally speaking, a brotherhood of all men, of all races and nations and creeds, in that all are the creation of God. It is a sort of human brotherhood in the flesh, and as such it gives evidence of all the failings that such a loose connection, with its many possibilities for disagreement and misunderstanding, would be expected to produce. A true brotherhood must be spiritual in nature, and be held together by spiritual ties. There is such a brotherhood. It is composed of those creatures who know God as Father, and have permitted themselves to be called sons of God because they believe the gospel of God as it is revealed in Christ Jesus, their Lord. This is the brotherhood that prays, "*Our* Father which art in heaven." It is a narrow brotherhood, but the most liberating brotherhood revealed to man.

The invocation to the Lord's Prayer, when seen as the truth about others, refers to this special brotherhood. Following Jesus' prayer to be glorified, in praying for the apostles and believers, he says, "I pray not for the world, but for them which thou hast given me; for they are thine." The world is not a brotherhood. The world cannot truly pray the Lord's Prayer. But the true brotherhood is not a closed group. Jesus also says, "Neither pray I for these alone, but for them also which shall believe on me through their word." The prayer touches the potentialities of those who will yet come into the fold. And how will these others come in? Through those who are already members of the brotherhood, and whom Christ sends into the world, even as God sent him into the world. The most convincing witness that those who know themselves to be sons of God can give the world is the practice of brotherly love among themselves. "By this shall all men know that ye are my disciples, if ye have love one to another." The task of world evangelization always comes back to the local congregation and individual Christians. If the spirit of brotherhood does not stand out in bold relief in the smaller groups of Christians, how will the world come to believe through them? There must be a stewardship of love.

We have been speaking only of the words, "Our Father." Jesus adds, "which art in heaven." This phrase further clarifies the picture of God which man must have in order to pray as he ought. It is not so much a matter of locating God, as the Hebrew people located Jehovah in their holy of holies. Locating is always a confining process. And God is not to be confined to any one locality. Rather, our approach to the phrase must be from the opposite angle. Heaven is where God is. It is not either here or there; not either now or hereafter. Jesus spoke of himself, it will be remembered, as being in heaven while he was yet on earth. If God is present with any particular congregation of Christians, that congregation is experiencing a bit of heaven. Accepting this as true does not imply, however, that heaven and earth are synonymous. Nor are they opposites. Heaven and earth are distinct, even as hell and earth are distinct. Earth is the void that may be filled with either heaven or hell, depending upon whether we admit or block God's presence. The most convincing evidence man can have of a heaven beyond this earth, where God dwells in His fullness, is his capacity to experience a bit of heaven while yet on earth. The same holds good with reference to hell.

These things interest us now with special reference to the prayer life. When we say, "Our Father which art in heaven," we begin to pray by addressing One who is great and holy, and who has power to bless. Such a beginning makes it necessary to set our minds on things above. Not above, as in a space relationship. Rather, we must set our hearts and minds on a level above a void earth, above the world that lies outside the true brotherhood of sons, above the passions and desires of mere creatures. We are about to have communion with God in heaven.

When we begin to pray, God must be our first thought. To hurry on to get to the problems before us, without first invoking the presence of God, is to invite failure. No solutions or blessings can be expected unless we can first say, in truth and in sincerity, "Our Father which art in heaven." Much has already come to us in the course of life, without our having sought after it—can God not grant us more? Humbly, we must entrust ourselves to God, believing that He "will give only good gifts to his children." And the greatest gift He can give to any child of His is a knowledge of Himself.

III. HALLOWING GOD'S NAME

"Hallowed be thy name." St. Matthew 6:9.

WE have seen that for him who would pray, the thought of God must be the first and predominant thought. And likewise, that the knowledge of God is prayer's greatest reward. It is not unnatural then, that in the Prayer of prayers, Jesus should make the first petition a petition for the hallowing of God's name. "Hallowed be thy name." Unless man's first desire is God's glory—unless he seeks above all else to keep God's person and character pure and holy in his own life, there is little point in asking for God's Kingdom, that God's Will be done in man, for daily bread, for forgiveness of sins, and for deliverance from evil. Seeking the things of God apart from God Himself is the place at which many prayers fail. Jesus, speaking out of rich prayer experience and Sonship, placed the first essential petition first.

It is commonly recognized that the background from which Jesus taught was the Hebrew religion. We thus have every right to assume that in referring to God's "name," he intended it to be understood in the same light as understood in the Old Testament. There it appears that "name" has reference to the revealed character of God. "And they that know thy name will put their trust in thee: for thou, Lord, hast not forsaken them that seek thee." "Some trust in chariots, and some in horses: but we will remember the name of the Lord our God." "The name of the Lord is a strong tower: the righteous runneth into it, and is safe."

But what is God's character, as revealed to us? He who set all things in order, giving them to partake of His own character, must Himself be orderly, which is to say: we can depend on Him. He is one who is displeased with our sin and profanity; who must allow the wicked to be trodden down by the fruits of their own folly; who will guard the ways of the righteous and restore the penitent soul. Is that not the substance of the prophets? He is revealed in history to be a God of righteousness, who allows the righteous nation to prosper and the ungodly to perish, thereby giving validity to the message of the prophets. He is revealed in nature as one who is benevolent when not profaned, and who will supply all the needs of man. He is revealed in Jesus Christ to be both manly and compassionate; both strong and tender; both stern and forgiving. And above all He is revealed as our Father in heaven, which thought has been previously elaborated upon. Surely this is the name that stood out most vividly in the mind of Jesus when he exhorted his disciples to pray, "Hallowed be thy name."

"Hallowed." It is a hard word. If we seek a definition, we find such phrases as "consecrated to a sacred

use," "treated as sacred." Our first petition is that
God's name be set apart from all things that are
unlike Him and out of harmony with His revealed
character and unworthy of His holiness. God's name
cannot be used lightly on the street, be made the
punctuation marks in conversation, be used falsely in
the court-room, and remain hallowed in the hour
of prayer. A name that is made common by continual
association with the trivial, by association with that
which is far removed from God, cannot be used effec-
tively in the moments when we communicate to
God in heaven our great need and dependence. It
may well be that God's name is more deeply profaned by the velvet phrases of those in high places
than by the wretched mortal whose vocabulary is so
poverty stricken as to prevent his emphasizing a statement without profanity. But if our race falls to a
lower level of culture and religion, it will not be
because of those in high places. It will be because the
multitudes have sinned against the Holy Ghost, and
severed prayerful communion with God by profaning
His holy name in thought, word, and deed.

There is but one garb in which the petition, "Hallowed be thy name," can be prayed. That is the garb
of humility—a humility which reminds its possessor
of his failings and needs. To pray in humility, which
is the exact opposite of self-glorifying prayer exemplified by the publican in Jesus' parable, is to
begin to hallow God's name. Many there are in the
world who are satisfied with themselves just as they

are. This is no prayer for them. The self-satisfied may be rich or poor, learned or illiterate, or in any conceivable condition. Self-satisfaction comes not from outer circumstances, but from inner hardness of heart. To pray, "Hallowed be thy name," is to admit that God is greater than self, that our lives are in His hands, and that is a humiliating experience to man who prides himself in having created a world of many comforts and luxuries. Yet this is the key petition to the treasures of God.

If this petition is answered in us, and the goal of our inner-most selves becomes the exalting, the reverencing, and the glorying in God's name, His name will be hallowed by our attitudes toward those things which are most clearly His. Of all the holy men who have traversed this old earth in human flesh, it goes almost without saying that Jesus Christ was the most definitely God's. As God incarnate, the name of Jesus Christ, the only begotten Son of the Father in heaven, merits equal position with that of God. He has for us the value of God. All that may be said relative to hallowing God's name applies with equal force to the name of Jesus Christ.

He, in whose heart the name of God is hallowed, will find the Bible to be the Word of God. It is one thing to know the history of the formation of the Bible, how certain books achieved their present form by the piecing together of various older traditions and manuscripts, what editorial hands they have passed through, and wherein various manuscripts

disagree. It is another thing to hear, speaking through
these Scriptures, the voice of the living God speaking to our own condition, whatever it may be. The
former may have scholastic merit, but the latter has
that which is more essential, spiritual merit. This
latter makes of the Bible a lamp unto our feet. The
possession of this conviction and attitude toward the
Bible sets the child of God free to study, without
fear, all that modern research reveals. The Bible is no
fetish. Possession of a leather bound copy will not
save any individual's soul. But its message, when
rightly received, can be a mighty force for righteousness. It will heap reason upon reason why God's
name ought to be hallowed.

He in whose heart the name of God is hallowed
will find the Church to be the body of Christ. He
will manifest reverence for God in the church, which
is His. But reverence for God is not necessarily expressed by attending all worship services of the congregation in which membership is held. It is not
necessarily expressed by partaking of the holy Sacra-
ment at specified intervals. It is not necessarily expressed by aiding the church's program financially.
These may be mere outer formalities, although they
need not be. For surely the humble heart which
looks beyond self to God whose name is hallowed in
heaven will put forth an effort to worship regularly
in the house of prayer, will gladly accept the bread
and the wine in the celebration of the Holy Communion, and will aid the church financially, ac-

cording as the Lord has prospered him. Reverence is not necessarily expressed by avoiding vulgar conversation in the church building, by quietness during the service, or by bowed head during prayer. These are outer acts which need not necessarily reach beneath the surface. But he in whose heart the name of God is hallowed will remember the high use to which the church building is dedicated, will be orderly during the worship of God, and will bow the head during prayer, for he will know from experience that the attitude of prayer is best maintained with bowed head.

He, in whose inner-most self the petition of our text is answered, will seek to conserve the wealth of nature, for to him the earth is God's footstool. He will see his fellowmen as either children or potential children of the heavenly Father, and love each one of them, even as Christ gave commandment. He will look upon his own person as the temple of the Holy Ghost, and not profane the sacredness of that temple. He will become less and less inclined to draw a sharp line between the sacred and the secular, for all that God has granted will begin to take on significance in the Divine Plan. "Hallowed be thy name." This must be our first and most urgent petition.

IV. THE COMING KINGDOM

"Thy kingdom come." St. Matthew 6:10.

WHEN we recall the great value placed by Jesus upon the Kingdom of God, it appears quite natural that, in the prayer bearing his name, the petition for the coming of the Kingdom should be given a prominent position. It is placed second to none save for the hallowing of God's name.

In beginning his ministry, Jesus proclaimed, "the kingdom of God is at hand." It is as though he were announcing the theme of his message. And truly the Kingdom is the key-note of his many discourses. The Kingdom is of first magnitude importance: "Seek ye first the kingdom of God." It is the hidden treasure: "The kingdom of heaven is like unto treasure hid in a field; the which when a man hath found, he hideth, and for joy thereof goeth and selleth all that he hath, and buyeth that field." It is the pearl of great price: "The kingdom of heaven is like unto a merchantman, seeking goodly pearls: who, when he had found one pearl of great price, went and sold all that he had, and bought it." The Kingdom is an eternal value which, when found by man, impresses its great desirability upon him with such vividness that he cannot be content until he is stepping out toward a more complete reception of it. As some stars in the heavens appear to out-shine other stars, so, in reality, the Kingdom out-shines all human joys and flickering satisfactions.

We have mentioned Jesus' announcing that "the kingdom of God is at hand." Yet we are taught to pray, "Thy kingdom come," implying thereby that the Kingdom is not fully come. At one time Jesus said, "the kingdom of God is within you." And at the last supper, we hear him saying, "I will not drink of the fruit of the vine, until the kingdom of God shall come," which makes the Kingdom a future hope. Like many truths, the great truth of the Kingdom can only be stated paradoxically. No precise definition of its position in time would be capable of containing it. We might play with words and say that the Kingdom exists eternally, in eternity, as opposed to existing in time. But for a workable understanding, we must return to the paradoxical presentation offered by Jesus. The Kingdom of God is both a present reality and a future hope. It is at this very moment the precious possession of unnumbered individuals. It is also something which these same individuals hope to greet at some future time.

And by whose initiative and power is the Kingdom come, and by whose initiative and power will it come at some future time? During times of material peace and prosperity we hear of man's building the Kingdom of God on earth. But when the affairs of earth turn toward war and material depression, we are more likely to hear that human effort is futile: God must Himself usher in the Kingdom. There is an optimism of prosperity that is sin, and a pessimism of depression that is likewise sin. The conditions of earth are in either case a temptation against which we ought to be on guard. We need the sobering realization that man cannot build the Kingdom of God. A kingdom built by men would be men's kingdom, rather than God's Kingdom. Men have built kingdoms in the past, they are building kingdoms today, and there is every reason to assume that others will be built in the future. Those of the past have fallen. Need any other word be added relative to present and future man-made kingdoms? No man, even though he be mad with genius, has an accurate blue-print of an enduring kingdom. No man, had he an accurate blue-print, would be capable of building such. God alone has such power. But we also need the invigorating realization that no efforts spent for the extension of God's Kingdom on earth are in vain. If we have faith in our Lord and trust his word, there will be no occasion to question the wisdom of his command, "Go ye into all the world." No man can possess the pearl of great price without having a desire to show it to others. No man can possess the Kingdom of God without the desire to share it with others. Even viewed from a selfish standpoint, the wisdom of Jesus' command is apparent. It is a truism that we learn a thing more thoroughly by teaching it to others. We likewise possess the Kingdom more fully by proclaiming its message to the ends of the earth. God alone is capable of ushering in His Kingdom, yet man must strive as though the reign of righteousness were his own responsibility.

The manner of the Kingdom's coming is summed up in two parables. God has taken the initiative. Man must be receptive. Then, when the Christ, sent of God, is received in human hearts, the Kingdom comes by a process of growth. "It (the kingdom of God) is like a grain of mustard seed, which a man took, and cast into his garden; and it grew, and waxed a great tree; and the fowls of the air lodged in the branches of it." There is steady growth. Jesus planted the seed in the hearts of his apostles. Through them others were received. And thus the process continues through the centuries, with each new generation, and each newly won portion of the earth adding to the branches thereof. Again, "It (the kingdom of God) is like leaven, which a woman took and hid in three measures of meal, till the whole was leavened." As the action of the yeast is gradually spread through all the meal, so the power of the Kingdom is gradually spread, through society perhaps, but more definitely through the whole of a person's life. Finally, our hopes and desires, our thoughts and deeds, are brought under the power of the Kingdom; and we shall be like our Lord.

But where will the Kingdom come? As for its present reality, it comes, as is made clear by Jesus' statement that "the kingdom of God is within you," in man. Being spiritual, it comes to man in spirit, and being received by man, is given bodily manifestation. Its light is not hid. Its fruits are seen by the world—although often not appreciated by the world, as in the case of Jesus when he was among his own people. As for its being a future hope, the Kingdom is a present reality in heaven. And in heaven there will be the complete fulfillment when the saints of all ages are gathered about the Throne. Of this there can be no doubt. But some will say, Cannot the future aspect of the Kingdom also apply to the establishment of the Kingdom of God on earth? Do we not look forward to the day envisioned by the prophets when man will study war no more?

Truly, we do long for that day, but the absence of war does not insure the Kingdom. I cannot help but feel that the hope for the Kingdom's being established on earth, when by that is meant a social and economic order embracing all mankind, is unfounded and totally futile. This in spite of the noble motives which often inspire such hopes—noble because those who thus hope admit that they will not live to see the fulfillment of their hope. Jesus said to Pilate, "My kingdom is not of this world: if my kingdom were of this world, then would my servants fight, that I should not be delivered to the Jews: but now is my kingdom not from hence."

We criticize the apostles for at one time entertaining the hope of an earthly kingdom. Should we fall into the same error? If any organization of men claims to be the Kingdom of God; if any nation of the earth claims to be the Kingdom of God; if at any time any league of nations should claim to be the Kingdom of God: we need only recall the gentle words of Jesus, "they shall say to you, See here; or, see there: go not after them, nor follow them." "The kingdom of God is within you."

And what is the Kingdom of God, and what will it be? It is the reign of God; the place where His character is constantly reflected. His reign is an eternal truth. The coming of the Kingdom is the manifestation of the reality which has always existed. God's reign may be manifest in us as individuals, and there will be a complete manifestation in heaven.

"Thy kingdom come." We pray that Jesus the Christ will come more fully into our hearts and be King of our lives, that we may have the joys of salvation and be the means by which others come to know the blessedness of citizenship. We pray that the kingdom of the world will become the Kingdom of our Lord and His Christ, and that we and all who join our prayer may have part in that final consummation.

V. GOD'S WILL IN US

"Thy will be done in earth, as it is in heaven." St. Matthew 6:10.

THE climax of the first division of the Lord's Prayer comes in the third petition. That which is at least partially implied in the preceding petitions is now given expression. "Thy will be done in earth, as it is in heaven." The petition, "Hallowed be thy name," has numerous implications in its own right, as does the petition, "Thy kingdom come." Yet it must be clear that if we truthfully desire the hallowing of God's name and the coming of His Kingdom, we cannot evade the longing for His Will to be done in us, and through us, and amongst ourselves.

When we here refer to God's Will, it is God's Will as concerns us, His children. The general phrase, God's Will, may have implications for the universe of nature, the stars, planets, and this earth. But these are of no direct concern to us in praying the Lord's Prayer. It is upon God's Will for men that our attention is focused. God's Will, like our human wills, is not arbitrary. It is not possible for us to place our thoughts and our feelings and our wills in separate compartments and direct them to function independently. When we act, it is the total personality that acts. That which we will is rooted in our thoughts and, more directly, in our feelings. Likewise, the Will of God is an expression of His total being—not of a separate and isolated division of Himself. The mind of God enters the picture. His perfect knowledge, which is the source of all truth, makes His Will for us just. God's feeling, if that phrase be permitted, which finds definition in the familiar words, "God is Love," makes His Will for us merciful. God's Will for men has its source, then, in His mind of Truth and in His heart of Love.

The nature of God's Will has not been left to human speculation, but has been revealed to us as a desire that we have eternal life. Too often the phrase "eternal life" is something hastily ushered out of this present life and made to be something far removed from present living. True, eternal life is a future hope, but it is also a present reality in the hearts of those who allow God to be King of their earthly lives, and thus are admitted to membership in the Kingdom. Eternal life has both quantity and quality. If our lives manifest those qualities which are eternal, the everlastingness of our lives will be of little immediate concern. It is God's Will that we, each one, have eternal life. Jesus, obedient to the Father's Will, came that we might have life, and have it more abundantly.

Obviously, there is much in the world that is contrary to the Will of God. Who would dare to say it is God's Will that bands of innocent hostages should be slaughtered in retaliation for the assassination of a single man in times of war? Who would proclaim a dreaded epidemic, leaving death and suffering in its wake, an act of the Will of God? A loved one, whose life was upright and beautiful, suffers severe torture in the closing moments of his life, but who is there so calloused as to credit that torture to the Will of God? We ask, Why? Volumes could be filled with the discussion of the problem of suffering. Yet no completely rational explanation is in sight. Jesus did not argue about why men suffer. He saw in suffering an opportunity to serve those in need. He carried healing to the diseased and sinful. Our wills are ours to make them God's. If this truth was more completely espoused by the children of men, much suffering that now is would never have come into being. And, on the other hand, much suffering that now is would be erased from the annals of current history. God's Will is not done in earth because man's will dares to aim its guns at God. "Men's hammers break—God's anvil stands."

"Thy will be done in earth, as it is in heaven." We pray that God will look upon our low estate and make of us instruments of His Will. That is a tremendous petition to offer. We who are sinful, and slow of understanding, and often rebellious, pray that we may be channels of God's Will. It is at once a confession that God's Will is not fully operative in us and through us and amongst ourselves, and the prayerful desire to have that which is in part become more consuming. In any consideration of obedience to the Will of God, its passive aspects must be noted, for these are present. The passive aspects are best illustrated by Jesus' prayer in Gethsemane: "O my Father, if it be possible, let this cup pass from me: nevertheless not as I will, but as thou wilt." Jesus was resigned to a bitter cup because it was the Father's Will. Few are spared a bitter cup, but those who drink all of it, assured that it is the Father's Will, find new beauties unfolded to them. The unfortunate commentary on this truth is that too often avoidable sufferings are credited to the Will of God —cups which God does not will men to drink. Those who are professing unbelievers point their finger and label religion an opiate. But they are blind, and their accusation is not true.

Active obedience is the dominant note. The phrase, "as it is in heaven," is added to make clear that this is the intention of the petition. In heaven there is no suffering or death. There God has wiped away all tears. It is clear, therefore, that in heaven obedience to the Will of God does not mean resignation to suffering and misfortune—there is no suffering or misfortune to be resigned to. Obedience there is living for God; it is living for the brotherhood. Therein is the key to the obedience for which we need most to pray; that our private egos may be consumed by the Will of God.

Praying the petition in this manner will mark a milestone on the road to true success. To have God's

Will, which cannot be divorced from His power, glow in us and through us will transform the impossible into the possible. War will become a thing of the past. Disease will be conquered. And men will be successful in pursuing their chosen vocations according to the talents of which they are stewards. Does this sound fanciful? Ah, the inventors of machines and the explorers of the earth sounded fanciful until they demonstrated the validity of their dreams. How much more do things of the spirit sound fanciful! Jesus assured the world that those who followed after him would accomplish greater works than those performed by himself. And he gave to men the prayer which is the means by which these greater works may be done under God. That which the world calls success today will look lame in the light of what success will mean when God's Will is done in earth, as it is now done in heaven.

Activity resulting from our being instruments of the Will of God will need increasing nourishment and knowledge. These God supplies. These come along with His answer to our petition. He is not a task-master, requiring bricks without straw. Response to the divine initiative produces the needed nourishment. "My meat (symbol of nourishment) is to do the will of him that sent me, and to finish his work." Response to the divine initiative produces the needed knowledge. "If any man will do his will, he shall know of the doctrine, whether it be of God, or whether I speak of myself."

But how is man to become sensitive to the Will of God? For surely it is clear that not all activity carried forth under the banner of God is in accord with His Will. A looking up to Christ as he is revealed in the Gospels will greatly aid in clearing our vision. We need to behold him in his infancy, in his temptation and conquest of evil, during his baptism and when he instituted the Holy Eucharist. We need to kneel before his cross, and feel the chill of his passion. We need to see him burst the bonds of the grave and feel the warmth of his resurrection. We need a vision of him sitting at the right hand of the Father. This we need, for Christ is the revelation of God's Will. Moments of silence in our secret prayer chambers will be broken by "the still small voice" offering us guidance. "Thy will be done in earth, as it is in heaven."

VI. OUR DAILY BREAD

"Give us this day our daily bread." St. Matthew 6:11.

WITH this petition we pass to the second division of the Lord's Prayer. In this portion of the Prayer the petitions are concerned with several more specific human needs. This is not to imply that the note of human need is absent in the first portion of the Prayer. Indeed, if God's name is not hallowed, His will not done in us, and His Kingdom receding rather than coming, then all petitions of human need are meaningless babble. Unless the necessity of the first three petitions is appreciated, there remain only animal needs, rather than human needs.

Of the several petitions of the Lord's Prayer, there is no other presenting greater difficulty of interpretation than the one for daily bread. Yet it is a petition which is near to the heart of every man; and rightly so. The difficulties, however, are of detail rather than of the essence of the petition. One difficulty is the word rendered "daily" in our Authorized Version. Various renderings have been suggested. Chief of these are "daily," "for the coming day," and "needful." "Daily" in the sense of that needed for today as opposed to some future time. "For the coming day" in the sense that the needs of the morrow will be provided on the morrow, or spiritualized to mean the day of the Kingdom. "Needful" in the sense of that which is necessary, as over against that which would be in excess of actual needs. The more one meditates on these possible renderings, the more clear it becomes that they represent unessential details. In all cases, the petition speaks of something which it is necessary for the one praying to have. The essence of the petition is, "give us our needed bread."

Another difficulty presents itself in the interpretation of the word "bread." The early Fathers spiritualized the word, believing it to mean the Bread of Life. A number of plausible arguments could be presented in defense of that position. Jesus desired for us life, and desired that we have it abundantly. He knew that man does not live by material bread alone, but by every word that proceedeth out of the mouth of God. To have only material bread leads to death. "Your fathers did eat manna in the wilderness, and are dead." Only the living bread of life, represented by Christ, can nourish a man for life eternal. Would Jesus be likely then to focus our attention on that which has no permanence? It is also to be noticed that if material bread is intended, the petition stands apart from the other petitions; it would seem to have little if any connection with what has gone before or that which follows.

On the other hand, one may say that when Jesus said "bread" he meant it to be understood literally as that which is necessary for physical life. Without material bread man cannot maintain his body, the temple of the Holy Spirit. God alone is able to supply the bread of physical life. To Him we must offer our petitions for that bread. "The eyes of all wait upon thee; and thou givest them their meat in due season. Thou openest thine hand, and satisfiest the desire of every living thing." Can God's name be hallowed or His Will done in and by men whose bodies are not nourished? Would an unfed body be a suitable habitation for the Kingdom of the Most High God? Without bread for the body man would be helpless to offer the prayer commanded by our Lord.

One may justify himself in holding to either of these two interpretations. But both are marked with the human weakness to make a thing mean either this or that. Yet, when we offer a petition to God, we must use words that have meaning to us. Without their having meaning to us, we would be guilty of offering vain repetitions. There must be a meaning true to the character of the prayer, sufficiently comprehensive not to be unduly narrow, and which will not do violence to any interpretation of detail which is justified. "Give us this day our daily bread." We pray for that nourishment which is necessary for abundant living; that food which will sustain the growth of the Kingdom of God in us. Obviously, the food necessary will consist of both food for the body and food for the spirit.

We need food, shelter, and clothing. Without these we become ill, and cannot live at all. The cells of the body die, and must be replaced by other cells. In the course of seven years we have a new body. If it is to be a healthy body, it must have available the food which insures health. There must be clothing and shelter to protect the body from that which without them would be the cruelties of the weather. Since in this world we are not a group of disembodied spirits, it may be said that our spiritual growth here is somewhat bound up with maintenance of our bodies. It is our privilege to ask of God material bread. It is, at the same time, our duty to keep the channels through which God supplies that bread open.

Likewise, we need what might be termed food, shelter and clothing for the soul. The soul needs food for nourishment. "My meat," said Jesus, "is to do the will of him that sent me." To do the Will of God as it is revealed to us in Christ Jesus, and as it is further clarified for us by communion with God, is to be built up in the true faith by which we are nourished unto life everlasting. The soul must be clothed as a protection against the storms of sin. St. Paul provides a most appropriate picture of this necessity: "Wherefore take unto you the whole armour of God, that ye may be able to withstand in the evil day, and having done all, to stand. Stand therefore, having your loins girt about with truth, and having on the breastplate of righteousness; and your feet shod with the preparation of the gospel of peace; above all, taking the shield of faith, wherewith ye shall be able to quench all the fiery darts of the wicked. And take the helmet of salvation, and the sword of the Spirit, which is the word of God." The soul needs the shelter of a home. The Church for which our Lord gave himself, and of which he is the ever living head, is such a home. To be outside the Church is to be a nomad soul without a spiritual home.

God is the source of all these benefits which nourish abundant life, and sustain the growth of the Kingdom in us. In these days many of us are far removed from agricultural pursuits. Our material food comes to us in such a round-about way as to make it easy for us to look upon ourselves as the source. Many work in offices, factories, or wherever, for which labor money is received. That money is taken to a store and exchanged for food or clothing produced at some distant point. The coin is in our pockets. We have earned it, we say—and it has oftentimes been literally by the sweat of the brow. But is not the frequent failure of many to look to God as the ultimate source another example of the necessity for religious growth keeping pace and going beyond material growth? To fail to see God as the source is to deny Him the throne of our hearts.

It may seem unlikely at first thought that there is a temptation to regard spiritual sustenance as from any source but God. There is a very real temptation to look upon self as the source of spiritual nourishment, and to it many yield. Think for a moment of the Pharisee who went up into the temple to pray. He "stood and prayed thus with himself, God, I

thank thee, that I am not as other men are, extortion-
ers, unjust, adulterers, or even as this publican." Two
things should be noted. He prayed "with himself,"
and that which he prayed was centered in himself.
Yet I dare say that the Pharisee was nearer the Kingdom than multitudes who make no gesture of men-
tioning God's name in prayer.

The job which we have is merely the channel
through which God supplies our material needs. The
channel may have to be changed from time to time.
But if by chance we see one channel closing, and do
not see another opening, what will be our frame of
mind? Will we dwarf our capacity to receive through
worry, or will we acknowledge God as the giver of
every good and perfect gift, and trust His power to
supply that which is needful? "Consider the lilies
how they grow: they toil not, they spin not . . . how
much more will he clothe you?"—you, who toil? Ah,
the channel through which God provides for our
physical needs may appear very strange at times.
The manna which God provided for the children of
Israel during their sojourn in the wilderness was very
strange to them.

The Church is the channel through which the
Bread of Life is supplied. To the world such a statement is foolishness. To those who have opened the
doors of their heart to the King, it is the Truth of
truths. Without the Church, not even the Holy
Scriptures can be considered a channel of spiritual
nourishment. It is a matter of historic fact that the

Church came first, and the Bible afterward. The Scriptures were delivered to the Church. To swear by the Bible and deny the Church is the height of folly —it leaves no ground to stand on. And to no body save the Church have valid sacraments been given, by which the promises of the Gospel are sealed to us.

It needs also to be stated that God, being righteous, supplies the needs of man through righteous channels. Man may possibly maintain physical life for a time by unrighteous means. But this is to eat damnation to oneself. The end is death; for man does not live by material bread alone. "Give us this day our daily bread," is a petition that exhibits trust in God's capacity to supply the necessities for growth in abundant living, and to nourish receptivity to the Kingdom of God.

VII. OUR DEBTS AND OUR DEBTORS

"And forgive us our debts, as we forgive our debtors."
St. Matthew 6:12.

ONE of the surprising facts about the Lord's Prayer is the manner in which each petition is bound up with all that has gone before, and the thoroughness with which it prepares us for that which is to follow. To petition God for forgiveness in proportion as we forgive others would be to call damnation upon our own heads, were it not for those petitions which precede it. And if at this point in the Prayer we yet find the petition difficult, its being difficult must stand as a judgment upon the lack of persistence demonstrated in our desire for God's Will to be done in us and His Kingdom to come into our hearts.

If this fifth petition were to be characterized apart from the other petitions, we might well call it the essential pause in prayer. On one occasion Jesus said, "And when ye stand praying, forgive, if ye have ought against any: that your Father also which is in heaven may forgive you." How often the Gospel brings us face to face with the necessity of forgiveness! Forgive! Forgive! The word rang in the ears of St. Peter. He came asking Jesus, "Lord, how oft shall my brother sin against me, and I forgive him?

till seven times?" Undoubtedly, St. Peter considered himself generous. Jesus saith unto him, "I say not unto thee, Until seven times: but, Until seventy times seven." And Jesus clearly teaches that our receiving from God the forgiveness which we so sorely need is bound up with the forgiveness granted by us to those who are our debtors. "All we like sheep have gone astray; we have turned everyone to his own way." Forgiveness by God is a necessity for all who would taste of Life. Forgiveness is the cure for the infection here termed debts.

But what are "our debts"? St. Luke's less familiar version of the petition reads, "And forgive us our sins; for we also forgive every one that is indebted to us." Our sins are the infection from which we suffer. Our sins render us debtors to God. "Debts" reminds us of our accountability to God. We have been unprofitable servants. On occasion we have wasted the talents entrusted to our keeping. On other occasions we have hid them in the earth. And realizing that there will be a day of reckoning, we plead that the debt be erased. Our debts are of two kinds: those resulting from sins of transgression; and those resulting from sins of omission. Obedience to the law of God as summarized in the Ten Commandments is binding upon all.

To willfully ignore, or, like sheep, wander away from these laws, is to be guilty of transgression. To our understanding of the Law must be added that additional light revealed by the Christ. Through him we have knowledge that the evil desire, and longing of the heart to be disobedient, is as much a transgression of the Law as the outward act. The clearer our vision of God, the greater our consciousness of guilt. Jesus, in revealing the Will of God, has given numerous positive commandments, all of which hang on the commandments to love God and to love our neighbors. To omit an act or word of kindness or of mercy of which we are capable through the talents entrusted to us by God is to have the sign of guilt placed upon us. "Lord, when saw we thee an hungred, or athirst, or a stranger, or naked, or sick, or in prison, and did not minister unto thee? Then shall he answer them, saying, Verily I say unto you, Inasmuch as ye did it not to one of the least of these, ye did it not to me." It is a searching condemnation for the sin of omission.

How necessary it is that we have forgiveness. Now forgiveness is, by its very nature, chiefly a matter of reconciliation. To be in sin is to be estranged from God; it is to be dead unto life eternal. It is doubtful if there is a more revealing word picture of those who are in sin than the simple statement that they are dead, and have no life in them. The forgiving father, speaking of the prodigal son upon his return says, "this thy brother was dead, and is alive again." One of the pitiable facts with which we are confronted in the world is that many creatures of God are dead and never awake to the blessedness of true life. "For the wages of sin is death; but the gift of God is eternal life through Jesus Christ our Lord." To be in sin is only to *earn* wages—and the wage is death. To accept forgiveness is to receive a gift of much greater value than even the wages of good works—it is to receive the gift of Life. Forgiveness means renewed life. It means the regaining of spiritual health. It is God's remedy for man's sin. "We know that we have passed from death unto life, because we love the brethren." There is the test. Those who are forgiven, love; and those who love, forgive.

The basis of forgiveness appears. It is a reciprocating process, undergirded by the sacrifice of Jesus Christ. We cannot be forgiven unless we forgive; nor can we forgive unless we are forgiven. "Forgive us our debts, as we forgive our debtors," is not a suggested order of advancement in the realm of forgiveness. We are members, one of another, in the body of Christ—the Church. Our functioning as members of that mystical body finds illustration in our own bodies. The body is healthy when supplied with essentials by the blood stream. And, on the other hand, a healthy body is necessary to make the essentials available to the blood stream. It is one reciprocating process. The process continues in operation because it is permeated with physical life, which life is the creation of God. In a somewhat similar manner, the members of the body of Christ forgive one another. But there must be something to make the process work. Such energy is available in God's forgiveness of the members. Viewed from the opposite angle,

God's forgiveness is not available unless our machinery of forgiveness is in gear. Of course, God's forgiving nature is not dependent upon us; rather, we simply cannot avail ourselves of His energy so long as we drift along in neutral. Again it must be said that the fifth petition speaks not of two processes, or of an order of advancement, but of one reciprocating process.

Nevertheless, after all this has been said, there remains an inescapable emphasis of condition upon the last phrase, "as we forgive our debtors." It must be so, for it is at that point where we usually stumble, throwing the reciprocating process out of gear. All who have injured us in some manner by transgressing our rights, or who have left us uncomforted when we were neighbor to them by virtue of our need and their talent to minister to that particular need, are to be forgiven. Forgiving and forgetting are not the same thing. There is a temptation to think that when a debt is forgotten it is forgiven. If it is only forgotten, we will in all probability remember it again should that same offender sin against us at a later time. True forgiveness wipes the page clean and leaves nothing to be remembered at some future time. We have suggested that love is the test for forgiveness. Now love, insofar as it is an emotion, gains its force from the will. As such it involves our sincere desires for the one loved, but does not necessitate any trumped up liking for the person involved. Love, even on the human level, does not consist of hugs and kisses; much less does it consist of these in the sphere of our religion.

God has ever been a forgiving God. He forgave the sins of penitent Israelites, whose sacrifices were as shadows of the more perfect sacrifice to come. With that more perfect sacrifice now having been offered on the Cross of Calvary, our hope of forgiveness centers on the Cross of our Lord Jesus Christ. "Who his own self bare our sins in his own body on the tree." Does that sound like a pious platitude? Sins are always forgiven by being borne by another. Among the members of Christ, the forgiver must write that which is forgiven on his own loss sheet. By bearing the sins of others we are released from both these and our own by God through Christ's sacrifice on the Cross.

This sin bearing becomes a reality in the Church. Seen as the body of Christ, the Church becomes the body of those who are members of Christ. This makes it unlikely that the world will find a means of experiencing forgiveness beyond the earnestness in which the Church conceives itself to be the sin-bearing body of the world. We must sacrifice for the Church if we would find security in the Church; we must bear the sin of the world if we would have forgiveness; we must proclaim the Gospel if we would have the joy of salvation. These things all fit together, and the Church becomes the means by which forgiveness is mediated on earth. Speaking to the disciples, who constituted the Church during Jesus' earthly ministry, our Lord does not mince words: "Verily I say unto you, Whatsoever ye shall bind on earth shall be bound in heaven: and whatsoever ye shall loose on earth shall be loosed in heaven."

If this world is to become a stronghold of righteousness, the children of God must be forgiven for the aggressive evil of not only the thief and the anti-social orator and the murderer, but of the ingenious men who direct the energies of the world toward constructing the kingdoms of Satan. The sin of the world is in our veins. Unless the children of God stand together as the body of Christ, both forgiving and seeking the forgiveness of God, there can be no healing for the nations. "Forgive us our debts, as we forgive our debtors."

VIII. DELIVERANCE FROM EVIL

"And lead us not into temptation, but deliver us from evil." St. Matthew 6:13.

DEPENDING upon the frame of mind one is in, this final petition may either appear natural, expressing an almost universal longing, or seemingly out of order, because of certain things we have been taught about temptation. We have been taught that temptation is good for us. Jesus was "led up of the spirit into the wilderness to be tempted of the devil." St. James tells us, "count it all joy when ye fall into divers temptations." Yet Jesus bids us pray, "And lead us not into temptation." Or one may ask, Does God really lead us into temptation? And if so, may it be that God tempts us? Again St. James says, "Let no man say when he is tempted, I am tempted of God: for God cannot be tempted with evil, neither tempteth he any man."

In praying the Lord's Prayer, we must be mindful of the fact that it is a carefully organized whole in which the subordinate divisions can be rightly understood only in terms of the whole, and in their relationship to other subordinate divisions. This final petition must be seen in the light of its following the petition for forgiveness. Prayer for forgiveness involves

the admission of sin. The remembrance of our misdoings is grievous to us. Knowing that we cannot of
our own merit pay the debt in which we have become
involved, we cry out to God for forgiveness. When
the cry is uttered in sincerity and faith, God hears
and abundantly pardons. To be pardoned causes one
to desire not to fall again into the sin that had formerly been burdensome. Thus it follows quite naturally that the forgiven should pray, "And lead us not
into temptation, but deliver us from evil." So guide us,
and strengthen us by thy forgiveness, that in the midst
of temptations we may stand, upheld by thy great grace.
May thy kingdom come into our hearts with such
reality, and thy will be so unmistakably done in us
that evil will have no power over us when temptations come, and we may be delivered from eating the
fruits of wickedness. It is difficult to determine on
which phrase the greater emphasis should be placed,
for each of the phrases aids in understanding the
other. To be freed from the craving to yield to temptation is to be delivered from subjection to evil. On
the other hand, to be delivered from evil is to be made
impervious to the darts of temptation. Yet neither of
these describes the present condition of the vast majority of us. These are descriptive, rather, of the
hoped for condition—the condition for which we are
invited to pray in this final petition.

Temptations, quite obviously, come to us through
two channels. They come to us from the world without, and from the world within ourselves. Beckoning

lights, and fine spun words, and the glitter of fool's gold, and the deceptive gayety of empty souls, meet us at every cross-roads. With hypnotic tinsels they seek to draw us into the empty death which they conceal. Satan, who according to tradition personifies the the forces of evil, knows all the tricks that demonic ingenuity has been able to conceive. Likewise, "every man is tempted," according to St. James, "when he is drawn away of his own lust, and enticed." The beast in us has never been completely conquered. Few there are who do not, from time to time, find him putting forth his ugly head, beckoning us to depart from the highway paved for our travel by the prophets, apostles, martyrs, and saints of all ages. And just so surely as there are temptations, so sure is it that back of them is the evil in which they have their source.

Evil, and the temptations which are its advance propaganda, are facts of experience. They are as old as Adam and Eve, and as new as tomorrow's news sheet. What we need to realize is that their coming to us does not of necessity make us corresponding sinners. Jesus was tempted in all things just as we are. I venture to say that his temptations were more and greater than ours because of his superior sensitiveness to good and evil. Yet he was without sin, having never yielded. But it must be noted that nothing which endangers the life of the soul is good for us. And no temptation that comes to us does, in the final analysis, endanger the life of the soul, as we shall see.

What then of God's role in this matter of evil and temptation? He, being Holy, does not tempt us or encourage us in the pursuit of evil. He does not desire that any should perish. Why should He, if such is true, and if He has authority over both heaven and hell, permit us to be tempted? Is it not that He desires for Himself men of strong character, rather than milk-fed puppets? If there be no opportunity to sin, what virtue could there be in righteousness of life? If there be no choices before us, how can character develop? With every means necessary for overcoming the lure of temptation and the power of evil having been made available through the grace of God, there can be no reasonable lament for the fact of temptation. Our prayer is for resistance and deliverance from tempta-tion and evil—the tares which God permits to grow along with the wheat until the harvest.

Such an interpretation of the facts places a tremen-dous responsibility upon man; a responsibility seem-ingly out of proportion to the inherent weakness of man. But man may become strong by casting his weak-ness upon God and permitting God, through Christ, to build him into the likeness of Christ, which is our reasonable and promised hope. The cross we are forced to bear or be crushed by is not shaped by God. It was not God who shaped the Cross upon which our Lord bled and died. But it was God who shaped Jesus after such a pattern as to enable him to bear that Cross victoriously. God will likewise mould us and build us up to such strength if we permit it.

Having knowledge of the fact of temptation and the kingdom of evil—one might add, from experience —Jesus raises this petition as a warning signal for man. He did not dispute the insight that temptation may be a means of grace, but he did recognize the possibility that temptation may also become the occasion for stumbling. In a familiar parable, Jesus refers to him who sowed tares among the wheat as "an enemy." In explaining the parable, he identifies the enemy as "the devil." We pray that the enemy, with all his cunning, may not gain control over us because of our looking to God for guidance. How essential is prayer in meeting the fact of temptation! Jesus, in Gethsemane, comes to his sleeping disciples and warns them, "Watch and pray, that ye enter not into temptation." The sleeping spirit is an easy mark for the fiery dart. Persistent prayer is a mighty shield.

> "In seasons of distress and grief
> My soul has often found relief,
> And oft escaped the tempter's snare,
> By thy return, sweet hour of prayer."

There is a striking similarity between the prayer offered by Jesus in Gethsemane and the petition which he has provided for our use. "O my Father, if it be possible, let this cup pass from me: nevertheless not as I will, but as thou wilt." The cup was a temptation in that it opened two possible avenues. One avenue was a back street through which Jesus might conceivably have escaped to physical safety at the peril of his soul. The other was a hard road that went past Golgotha and on to victory. The call of duty to God and man was clear, yet it was a terrifying temptation. "O my Father, if it be possible, let this cup—this temptation—pass from me." "And lead us not into temptation." "Nevertheless not as I will, but as thou wilt." My desire may be in error. If this temptation must remain with me, then grant me grace to turn my back to the lower choice; the choice that leads to the realm of evil. "But deliver us from evil."

Our praying the Lord's Prayer has brought us to a high hurdle beyond which can be seen the open door to Life with God. In spite of all our good intentions and well formed plans, we are confronted with this final hurdle of temptation. Standing so near the goal of victory, we find ourselves in a new atmosphere where sin is seen as the fiendish thing that it really is. Coming now to a better understanding of sin and its consequences, we are less likely to be attracted to it. The tinsel of temptation becomes corroded before our very eyes. And in answer to our petition, we are enabled to scale the hurdle of temptation and enter in at the open door of Life. For as has been said, there is no temptation that can endanger the soul of those who trust not in their own weakness, but in the strength of God. "God is faithful, who will not suffer you to be tempted above that ye are able." Even the tempter must be obedient to the voice of God, and therein lies our sure hope.

IX. AN ESSENTIAL OF TRUE PRAYER

"For thine is the kingdom, and the power, and the glory for ever." St. Matthew 6:13.

ALL prayer that is worthy of the name ought, in spirit, to ascribe these things to God, for they are truly His and not our own. The thought contained in this ascription is an essential that ought to be present in every prayer, whether that prayer be for self, for others, or thanksgiving to God. And although it need not always be expressed in so many words, it is nevertheless good to use the words in order that we may be thereby more deeply impressed with their significance, and further prompted to make them a part of our innermost thoughts.

We also recall that Jesus exhorted us to pray in his name. This is again something which may be given verbal expression or not. It has become customary to close prayers with an appropriate phrase embodying that thought. It needs to be remembered, however, that the mere use of the words does not insure that the prayer has been in his name. On the other hand, a prayer could be offered which would truly be in his name without the use of the words. Yet there is value in using the phrase, "through Jesus Christ our Lord," or some similar phrase, because we are thus reminded of how we ought to pray.

When we come to know Jesus, who is called the Christ, prayers offered in his name are free from all selfish motives, even as he himself was free from all selfish motives. So free from selfish motives, and saturated with divine love was he that he gave his life on the cursed tree for the life of the world. "Greater love hath no man than this, that a man lay down his life for his friends." "I am the good shepherd: the good shepherd giveth his life for the sheep." But probably a distinction ought to be made between selfish desires and desires for those things essential to self. Things necessary for the highest development of the individual, and which enable him to be more efficient in rendering his particular service to the world, in a more acceptable manner, ought not, when desired in the spirit of the Christ, be counted as selfish desires. A selfish desire might be characterized as one divorced from the intention of rendering a proportionate service; the desire for something to be gained to the disadvantage of another, and the other to be hindered thereby in gaining a just advancement; a desire for self which knows no love for brother and which if granted would add to the worship of self by subtracting from the worship of God. This latter suggests a key question: Will the desired thing inspire greater dependence upon God, or detract therefrom?

Surely, a prayer growing out of a selfish desire has little possibility of being efficacious. It is against the possibility of the petitions of the Lord's Prayer being offered in a selfish manner, out of harmony with the spirit of Christ, that the ascription, "For thine is the kingdom, and the power, and the glory, for ever," acts as a safeguard. If the kingdom—the entire realm of the material, mental and spiritual in which we are given to have part—is recognized as God's, and the power by which the kingdom comes to us is recognized as God's rather than our own, and God is given the glory for the result these work in our lives, rather than desiring for ourselves the glory of men, we will be truly praying in the name of Jesus Christ our Lord, whether we add the phrase or not.

Not all of the potentially good things which come to us in the course of life, either as a result of prayer or otherwise, will automatically be good for us and add to our best interests. That which might be to one the key to abundant life could just as easily be to another a chain binding him to the earth or dragging him into the quick-sands. The character of the individual is the determining mill that grinds the good things of life into either keys or chains. Physical comforts, for example, may be to one the factor allowing him to be more useful to the world, permitting him greater freedom and opportunity for enriching humanity according to his particular gifts and capacities; to another, physical comforts might be the instruments by which he would be drawn in more upon himself and, with lack of industry, become a liability to the world instead of an asset. The ascription which brings the Lord's Prayer to a conclusion is the light by which man may see to walk upright amid the good things bestowed upon him. The darkness of its absence causes him to stumble.

"Give, and it shall be given unto you . . . For with the same measure that ye mete withal it shall be measured to you again," are not idle words having a pious sound, but of no practical worth. Their implications are transferable to the thought of our text. Finally, we will have for ourselves only that which we give into the hands of God. If God's Name is to be for us a hallowed name, we must recognize the fact that it is His Name, and is not hallowed because of anything in us for which we are ourselves responsible. If God's Kingdom comes to us, it is of His initiative and not through any merit of our own, much less through any building of it by ourselves. If God's Will is done in us, it must be acknowledged to be God's Will rather than our own, our own wills being too fragile for anything nearly so splendid. Our daily bread is as much the possession of God given for our nourishment as was the manna in the wilderness, for we cannot of ourselves so much as make a grain of wheat. Forgiveness, if it is really experienced, comes of God's grace, which grace exists regardless of our accepting it, and is not the result of our earning it by forgiving our fellowmen—we, whose transgressions outnumber the sands of the sea! Deliverance from evil comes of God's love and not of our lifting ourselves, by our own boot-straps, above the mire. Were God's guidance to be severed from man, all distinctions between salvation and damnation would cease to exist.

Said Jesus, "without me ye can do nothing." Whatever our petitions be, that which they bring to us must be acknowledged to be the Lord's, and must be permitted to remain in His sustaining care. Again it must be said, We retain only that which is given into the hands of God.

"Thine is the kingdom." We are not our own. It is not given to us to choose which are the forbidden fruits and which the permitted. The fruits of the earth are His, for He made them. The life entrusted to our living is His, for it is of His breath. All things of earth and sea and sky; all things of body, mind, and soul are His. We waive all claim to their possession. "Thine is the kingdom." And then we are led into green pastures, and beside still waters.

> Thine is the Kingdom,
> Thine alone —
> No merit breathes
> In my heart of stone;
> The life that living
> Appears to be me,
> Is naught but a shadow
> Of that which is Thee.

"Thine is the power." We are weak, but He is strong. It has not been given unto us to produce life, how much less can we fathom rebirth. He who has set the firmament on high has power over the substance of the kingdom and over our availing ourselves of the same. We waive all claim of power to build utopias. We lay down human hopes of waging war on heaven, and thereby gaining entrance to its splendors. "Thine is the power." And then God draws us unto Himself by the magnetism of the Cross.

> Thine is the Power,
> Thine to wield
> The germs of life
> In sky and field.
> Thine is the Power
> To lift me up,
> To spread the feast
> Where I with Thee sup.

"Thine is the glory." Unto Him whose the Kingdom is, and by whose power were all things made that were made, belong also the praise and the glory. No longer do we seek our own glory; there is One to whom glory is due.

> Thine is the Glory
> Now and ever —
> May no selfish thought
> Me from Thee sever;
> Thanksgivings rise
> From me to Thee —
> Thine is the Glory.
> Thus must it be.

And in the words of St. Jude, "Now unto him that is able to keep you from falling, and to present you faultless before the presence of his glory with exceeding joy, to the only wise God our Saviour, be glory and majesty, dominion and power, both now and ever. Amen."